BOOK OF THE DUMB 2

Uncle John's PRESENTS

BOOK OF THE DUMB 2

JOHN SCALZI

Portable Press
San Diego, California

UNCLE JOHN'S PRESENTS
BOOK OF THE DUMB 2

Project Team
Amy Briggs, Editor
Allen Orso, Publisher
JoAnn Padgett, Director, Editorial and Production
Michael Brunsfeld, Cover Design
Kaelin Chappell, Interior Design
Susan Gerber, Composition and Layout

For information, write
Portable Press
5880 Oberlin Drive, San Diego, CA 92121
e-mail: unclejohn@advmkt.com

ISBN: 1-59223-269-8

Library of Congress Catalog-in-Publication Data (applied for)
Printed in the United States of America
First printing: October 2004

04 05 06 07 08   10 9 8 7 6 5 4 3 2 1

DEDICATION

This book is dedicated to Dora and Mike Blauser, my in-laws,
because this is the only way either of them
would ever show up in a book like this.
Much love to the both of you.

CONTENTS

ACKNOWLEDGMENTS

This is the second book in the *Dumb* series, and I'm pleased to note that it was as much fun the second time around as it was the first time (how often can you say that about anything?). Here are some of the people who helped to make it so.

First, big thanks to my Beta Readers, who took a look at the raw articles and offered grammar and story suggestions. Most particularly, thanks to (in no particular order) Richard Jones, Duncan McGregor, Zeynep Dilli, Dave Ciskowski, Tony Dismukes, David Hodson, Christopher Nelson, Kevin Hicks, Laurel Halbany, and Aaron Brown. Once again, I'm sure a few names have slipped my mind—I beg forgiveness.

Much of the research for this book was done via the Internet—an obscure computing network that many people don't know about, but which I think will be big one day. You heard it here first. Yet again, the site that was the biggest help in gathering stories was FARK.com, whose tireless band of Farkers post crazy stories of people doing insane things at all hours of the day and night. To proprietor Draw Curtis and his merry crew, I reiterate my claims of much rockage. France surrenders. Your dog wants steak. Still no cure for cancer. Many thanks.

At Portable Press, editor Amy Briggs was paid to put up with me, and I'm sure they didn't pay her enough for what I put her through. Many thanks to her for giving the book structure and focus. Thanks also to JoAnn Padgett, Allen Orso, Kristen Marley, and Mana Monzavi, fine people all.

My wife Kristine and daughter Athena make this universe a better place to be in, and whenever I marveled at the absolutely inane things people do with themselves, as I of course frequently did in writing this book, it was nice to be able to look to them for counterbalance. All my love to them, today, tomorrow, and on and on.

PREFACE

Welcome to the world of the dumb. Again.

In this second foray into a place where bizarre events occur, the odd is commonplace, the eccentric is everyday, the weird is a walk in the park, and people definitely DO do the strangest things in the strangest places—they still all share one thing in common. No matter what the occasion or location—when these folks came to the party, they all checked their brains at the door.

Thanks to the verbal prestidigitations of John Scalzi, Uncle John's very own ringmaster of the absurd, we think that their faults, foibles, mistakes, and misdemeanors make for some pretty darned interesting reading. Sit back, relax, and read all about:

- Setting off fireworks, indoors;
- Mixing polar bears and cookies;
- Drinking mystery fizz from chemistry class;
- Breaking out of jail for a beer run; and many, many more!

These stories are like potato chips; bet you can't read just one . . . and we hope you enjoy them down to the last crumb. They're a no-fat, zero-carb snack for your brain.

Bon appetit,
Uncle Al
Publisher

INTRODUCTION

I'm going to let you all in on a secret: When writing a book like *Book of the Dumb 2*, the question is not: *Will I find enough stuff to write an entire book?* The question is: *Aaaaaugh! There's too much stuff! What do I choose?*

It's no joke. Every day during the writing of this book there would be eight, ten, or even twelve stories I'd read that would be a truly excellent fit for *Book of the Dumb 2*. It's an embarrassment of riches. This is good for us, the people who make the book, but at the same time it also makes us wonder about the sort of world we're living in. Well, we'll let someone else bother with the philosophical and sociological ramifications of such an avalanche of dumbosity. For us, and for this book, we just want to have fun with it all.

And so: *Book of the Dumb 2,* with its stories lovingly handpicked for their extra special dumbness. I'm proud to say that once again, the stories and the people in them run the gamut, from common thieves to uncommon celebrities, from the very smart (who should know better) to the very, well, *not* smart. As I mentioned in the introduction to the first book, it's not just "stupid" people who do dumb things. Everybody does them. They are the great leveler in our world. Dumb moves are perhaps the most democratic expression of the human condition we have. Also, they're good for a laugh. You can't beat that.

Those of you who are picking up this book without having read the first *Book of the Dumb* don't need to worry—this book is self-contained, so jump right in and enjoy it. Those of you who *did* read the first *Book of the Dumb,* however, will notice a couple of changes. Most obviously, the book is now arranged by chapters—so if you want to just read stories about people behind the wheel or getting stupid with fire, you don't have to hunt through the book: they're all in one place for you. And there are other new bits as well:

- **Dim Bulbs In Bright Lights:** A collection of films featuring famously dumb characters: From Jeff Spicoli to the dudes from *Dude, Where's My Car?,* all your favorite cinematic idiots are here.

- **The Annals of Ill-Advised Television:** You know how every year, there are some TV series where you just look at them and think: *how on earth did THAT get on the air?* This is a celebration of those shows. We've got shows that should have killed off the whole broadcast medium, yet somehow strangely did not.

All of this on top of favorite features from the first book: The Really Stupid Quizzes, and Tips for Stupid Criminals. And of course, many, many tales of dumbness that you have every right to expect from a book entitled *Book of the Dumb 2.*

Have fun with the book, and remember: don't *ever* let any of these things happen to you.

Enjoy!

—John Scalzi

CHAPTER 1

BiG DUMMY
ON CAMPUS

Higher Education—they say it's about making everyone smarter, but the following adventures seem to indicate otherwise. So sit back and thrill to the adventures of the following collegians, who while they may not graduate *Summa Cum Laude,* may graduate *Summa Cum Dummy,* if they graduate at all. And for all you folks in college right now: do any of this stuff, and your folks will instantly cut off your tuition. And that would be pretty darn terrible.

THE GREATEST SCAVENGER HUNT IN THE UNIVERSE

There are scavenger hunts, and then there are scavenger hunts. And then there is the annual University of Chicago Scavenger Hunt, the biggest, baddest hunt of them all. Nationally recognized, every year the judges of the scavenger hunt—part of an official student group at the university—present a list of some of the strangest objects and most bizarre tasks that humans can legally find or do. Students from the University of Chicago then get them or perform them in front of judges. The whole shebang takes just three days, but the side effects last a lifetime. Below you'll find some choice selections from recent U. of C. Scavenger Hunt lists. You have to be smart to do stuff this dumb:

- Find the tallest person you can find. Seriously. As simple as that. The team that presents the judges with the tallest person gets the points. Also, throw in the hairiest chest, the biggest ears, the longest tongue, the worst tanline, the webbedest toes, the longest eyelashes, the most nipples, the longest hair, the longest nails, and the most different-colored eyes. Everything must be real, and it goes without saying that bonus points are awarded if one person has all of these aesthetic features.

- At the sound of the whistle, load your mouth with sunflower seeds. Get the kernels on the inside and save them somewhere in your mouth. After five minutes the person with the most unbroken kernels and no shells in their mouth is the winner.

- Find an out-of-order sign that is out of order. No infinite regressions.

- Welcome Sam Ertal of the Pennington High School to the U. of C. class of 2008 with a singing telegram. Face to face. (Poor Sam!)

- "Hand-sync" Billy Joel's "We Didn't Start the Fire," in sign language, five people max, live performances (accompanying the not-live song) only.

- Build a working Erector-set model of the reproductive system.

- Locate a urinal coffee cake. (Use your imagination.)

- Do a handstand while wearing a helmet affixed to (as many as possible) those cups that make a sound of a bleating sheep when inverted.

- Cynics of the world unite—sculpt a hammer and sickle entirely out of press-on nails.

- Get your mitts on a pop-up book featuring a knife-fight, heroin overdose, bombing, and cannibalism, you know, for the kids.

- Slice a banana before peeling it. Don't destroy the peel or banana.

- Create a meal that breaks the rules of as many religions as possible. Provide textual evidence of the rules, and the judges mean primary sources.

- Eat one Krispy Kreme glazed doughnut in ten seconds. You have one try. You have no milk. (No mention of coffee though. Hmmmmm.)

- Bring a tire. On it, fit as many team members as you can. In diapers.

Source: http://scavhunt.uchicago.edu

STUPIDITY IS ALIVE AND WELL AND WEARING GREEK LETTERS

Through the years, America has always turned to its fraternities as the frontline laboratories for incomprehensibly stupid acts. Be it swallowing goldfish, jamming pledges into telephone booths, or setting new records in the highly competitive field of undergraduate emergency stomach evacuations due to alcohol poisoning, everyone breathes a little easier knowing that the boys in the frats are hard at work.

But then came the last couple decades, and universities cracked down on undergraduate stupidity. In these uncertain times, could fraternities be relied upon to maintain the noble tradition of rampaging stupidity that is their very birthright?

The answer comes from the University of Missouri–Columbia chapter of Kappa Alpha. Among the various accouterments of the KA house was a cannon, which according to legend dated back to Civil War times. The cannon hadn't seen much action recently—the Civil War is long over, even in Missouri—and some of the brothers apparently thought this was a real shame. The boys didn't happen to have any cannon shot or black powder handy (there's never a cannonball around when you need one), but they did happen to have fireworks. Lots of fireworks. Because what's a fraternity without colorful explosives? The boys from Kappa Alpha stuffed that Civil War-era cannon full of fireworks and let her rip.

So what happened? Well, for starters, the cannon's not there any more. Well, *parts* of it are. But other parts of the cannon were flung across the street and into an apartment complex, blowing out windows, tearing holes into floors and ceilings, and destroying various objects. Chunks of metal were also embedded into the brick of the apartment complex. Fortunately no chunks of metal were embedded into human beings, either at the fraternity house or the apartment complex, but that probably has more to do with luck than anything else.

The national organization of Kappa Alpha, which was shocked, *shocked* to discover stupidity going on at one of its chapters, immediately suspended the Missouri–Columbia house and noted on its Web site that the chapter's president and vice president were facing charges. Kappa Alpha also noted it would be conducting its own investigation. We understand double-secret probation will not be on the plea bargaining table.

Source: Associated Press, Kappaalphaorder.org

IF NOTHING ELSE, HE HAS A DEGREE IN CHUTZPAH

Remember the golden age of Internet plagiarism, when you could just go online and cut-and-paste willy-nilly for whatever paper you were writing at the moment? Yeah, well, it's been over for, like, a couple of years now. Most seem to have caught on to either that a) it's morally wrong or b) college professors can use Google.com just as well as anyone, so this bit of news should come as no surprise. But there are always stragglers.

Like "Ben," a student at the University of Kent in Canterbury, UK. The day before Ben was going to get his degree in English, he was informed that in fact, his diploma would be withheld, on account of Ben's plagiarism. Apparently the University of Kent is under the opinion that if you don't actually write your papers, you shouldn't get credit for them. How wacky!

Ben's response was to sue. He didn't deny he rampantly plagiarized—indeed, the results would have been grim if he had—but he claimed he was never told plagiarism was, you know, bad. "I can see there is evidence I have gone against the rules," Ben said. "If they had pulled me up with my first essay at the beginning and warned me of the problems and consequences, it would be fair enough. But all my essays were handed back with good marks and no one spotted it." In other words, Ben shouldn't be penalized because he managed to get away with breaking the rules for so long.

University officials noted that there were places where the university clearly spelled out that plagiarism was a naughty thing to do—for example, in the university handbook, issued to all students, as well as the English department's handbook, provided to all students who majored in that subject. In other words, to borrow a phrase from the geek world, this is another case of "RTFM," short for "Read the Freakin' Manual." One ought to be able to expect at least that much out of an English major.

Source: BBC

HOW TO BECOME THE MOST HATED MAN iN COLLEGE PARK

It's not often that a college student will actually want to go out of his or her way to become the most unpopular person on campus. But if it's the weekend and you don't have anything better to do, you can follow the path of "Brad" of the University of Maryland, College Park, campus.

As a bit of background, the university had a computer program called Direct Connect, which allowed people all over the Maryland computer network to share files (and by "share files," you can understand this to mean "massive egregious copyright violations as every student on the network swaps music and movies with everyone else"). The University of Maryland has sternly warned the students on the network that if copyright holders chose to sue them, that the students were on their own.

Well, as a prank, Brad—by all indications a devotee of the file sharing system himself—sent out a note to some friends saying that he'd tipped off the suits at the RIAA (the music industry watchdog group who is famously suing downloaders left and right) of all the copyright violations on Direct Connect. The e-mail, it turns out, was a prank. Ha! Ha! Ha! Brad, in fact, never alerted the RIAA at all. However, the Maryland student who ran Direct Connect on the Maryland network was not aware that the e-mail was all good, clean, geeky fun. And so, he shut down Direct Connect, depriving 25,000 undergraduates and 10,000 grad students of their infinite jukebox and cineplex.

It doesn't take a genius to figure out that Brad instantly became the most hated man in College Park once news of the failed joke got out. All over campus, fliers went up that said "Can't Get on Direct Connect? Say Thanks to Brad." They included his picture, his e-mail address, IM sign-on, physical address, and phone number. He received tons of threats and hate mail; Brad even filed an assault complaint after he was pushed around a bit. Let's just say until the whole thing got cleared up, Brad probably spent a lot of time under his bed and not answering the banging at his door. We also don't expect he'll be going back for reunions.

Brad's lesson—on the whole, people love pranks, especially when they involve a cow. But mess with their "free" music and movies? They'll hunt you down and kill you. Really, a lesson for us all.

Source: *Baltimore Sun,* DiamondbackOnline.com

A DOUBLE-ENTENDRE
THAT HAS ABSOLUTELY
NOTHING TO DO WITH SEX

Did you know that in England, a "flashlight" is known as
a "torch"? We're not exactly sure why that is—after all,
there was a perfect good meaning for the word "torch" already,
namely, "that stick with fire on the end." But you know the
British. Just because they *invent* a language they think they
know how to *use* it. Anyway, remember this little fact about
flashlights.

Now, come with us to England, where "Brian," a student
at Bath Spa University College (speaking of odd language
structure—Bath Spa University College? Does everyone there
major in redundancy?) had lost his shoe. He knew it was
somewhere in his room—probably under his bed—but he
couldn't see it anywhere. He peered under his bed, but it was
dark under there. He needed some extra light. "I didn't have a
torch but I had a lighter and I used that," Brian later told the
local newspaper.

Now, let's review what we have so far: a cigarette lighter,
which while indeed illuminating, is also an open flame. This
open flame was then thrust under a bed, made up of a flammable mattress (and possibly an equally flammable box-
spring), into a space filled with dust bunnies, shoes, and other
kindling-like objects. Not an ideal spot for an open flame at all.

Put all of that together, and suddenly he had a hot time
under the bed, and not the *good* kind of hot time. No, we're
talking *actual* fire. Brian and his roommates tried to douse

the flames, but the smoke got to them and they vacated the premises. Brian ended up burning his room to a crisp and otherwise causing structural damage to the house he and his roommates rented.

So, if we were in jolly old England, we could say, in amusingly arch fashion, if only Brian had had a torch, he wouldn't have torched his house.

Source: *The Chronicle* (Bath, UK)

The Really Stupid Quiz
BiG DUMMY ON CAMPUS

One story is true—two are false. Pick the right one, and you'll have received your BA in BS detection. Miss it, and you'll have to go back for yet another year of lazy college days, intermittent classes, and all the partying you can stand. Yeah, we know. Not much incentive to get it right, is it?

1. Two Emory University undergraduates were sent to the emergency room after playing a new drinking game for several hours. Described in the university's student newspaper, the *Emory Wheel,* the game, called "The Online Dating Clichés Chug-a-Lug," is played similarly to the television drinking games in which alcohol is consumed whenever a TV character says one of his or her stock phrases. In the online dating game version, students log into an online dating service, cruise through the profiles, and drink whenever common clichés arise (i.e., "Looking for new adventures" instead of "newly-divorced") and when dubious titles appear in the Favorite Books and Favorite Movies categories. Sartre and Godard are immediate signals to chug, according to the article.

2. An administrator of the University of Canberra, Australia, got his knickers in a bunch when a quartet of men he thought were burglarizing his home turned out to be students. The students had broken into the home of university vice chancellor and president Roger Dean and were ruffling

through his wardrobe when police arrived to make the arrest. The students were participating in a school-wide scavenger hunt being run as an adjunct to a fund-raiser for school charities; objects on the scavenger list included "the pyjama bottoms of at least one university administrator." "If they'd have asked, I would have cheerfully handed them over," Dean said. "But having them mysteriously appear in my home was somewhat distressing." Canberra police initially arrested the four on attempted burglary charges but released them after Dean declined to press charges.

3. The two art students from the Czech Republic wanted to make sure their creative efforts would be noticed—it was the end of the term and so they needed their work to go off with a real bang. And so the two cobbled together two objects made out of old electronic components, slapped stickers on them which said "EXPLOSIVE," and then dropped them off in the city center of Brno, one of the Czech Republic's largest cities. Well, the effort *was* noticed; the city center shut down for hours while bomb disposal experts fiddled with artworks. The police came after the students and charged them with conspiring to cause a public disturbance. Who turned them in? Their professor. Guess they shouldn't be counting on that "A" after all.

Turn to page 329 for answers.

Dim Bulbs in Bright Lights
DUMB AND DUMBER (1994)

Welcome to Dim Bulbs in Bright Lights, a celebration of some of the best dumb characters in film. You don't have to be dumb to enjoy dumb characters—in fact, it helps if you're not.

Our Dumb Guys: Lloyd Christmas (Jim Carrey) and Harry Dunne (Jeff Daniels)

Our Story: Two big-hearted but essentially brainless guys hit the road in their shaggy dog-shaped van to drive cross-country and return a misplaced suitcase full of money to its rightful owner, Mary, a woman (Lauren Holly) in trouble with a couple of thugs and with whom Lloyd falls in love. Hilarity ensues.

Dumb or Stoned? Clean livers both, Lloyd and Harry are just plain dumb. The closest these two come to taking drugs occurs when Lloyd takes revenge on Harry, who he believes stole his girl, by slipping him a mugful of laxative.

High Point of Low Comedy: On their road trip across the country, Harry and Lloyd use a container to relieve themselves in the car. Unfortunately, a state trooper pulls the two over and mistakes this open container for beer and not pee. That's a taste test he won't ever forget.

And Now, In Their Own Words: Lloyd has just traded in their nice big van for a teeny moped, and Harry says: "Just when I thought you couldn't get any dumber, you go and do something like this . . . and totally redeem yourself!"

They're Dumb, But Is the Film Good? Not really. But it *is* an acknowledged classic of the "Effluvia and Stupidity" comedy genre, so if you're a big fan of poo jokes, it's a must see.

CHAPTER 2

BLAME IT ON THE FAME

Look at it this way: everybody does dumb things. We do. You do. Even hugely famous stars do. But most of the time, when regular people do something a little dippy, the paparazzi isn't waiting in the bushes to try to snap pictures of the event and sell them to the highest bidder. (Sometimes obscurity is a good thing.) But just because celebrities are easy targets, they still don't get a pass. Clearly, any sympathy for the rich and famous only goes so far.

NOT EXACTLY
A "SMOOTH CRIMINAL"

We can believe that formerly beloved and now mostly inexplicable celebrity Michael Jackson has an aversion to being identified—honestly now, given his personal history over the last several years, if you were him, would *you* want to be identified? Jackson's problem is that his attempts to be "low-profile" end up being pretty obvious. If a skinny man of indeterminate skin tone comes toward you wearing both a surgical mask and a jacket with sequins and epaulets, who else is it going to be? And when he's not being obvious, he's simply scaring the townsfolk.

Case in point: February 2004, Michael Jackson is in Colorado with his children when he decides that what he really needs to do is visit the Wal-Mart located in West Glenwood Springs—apparently Jackson, like many Americans, is all about value. But of course Jackson is concerned about being mobbed by the fans, so he decides to enter the store incognito. "Incognito" in this case meaning "while wearing a ski mask."

Well, as most people know, wearing a ski mask into a commercial establishment that's *not* directly adjacent to a ski slope is the universal symbol for "Hello! I'll be your robber for today." So the good news is that the Wal-Mart employees and customers did not realize that Michael Jackson was in their midst. The bad news is that they thought they were being robbed. And the last thing Michael Jackson needs at this point is to be confused with a criminal, smooth or otherwise.

The employees called the police, who arrived after Jackson had left the store, but who then questioned Jackson a short time later in his vehicle, which had been described to the cops by the Wal-Mart employees. Interestingly, this wasn't the first time that week that Jackson had frightened the water out of a retail worker; Jackson pulled the same "ski mask" trick at a camera shop in Aspen, causing an employee to note, "When he first came in, I thought we were being robbed." The employees at the Aspen Sharper Image store didn't think they were being robbed, but as one noted: "I had no idea it was him, but I did think it was a bit strange for someone to be wearing that outfit."

Source: TheDenverChannel.com

RUB & ROLL

Here's what you do when you spend a boatload of money to acquire a guitar signed by one of your all-time guitar heroes. When you get it, first you take pictures of yourself with the guitar, in a rock god pose, fake pinwheeling your arms like Pete Townsend or hammering the frets *à la* Eddie Van Halen. And then, once you've had your fun, you mount it on your wall like a prize marlin and you *never touch it again*. To do otherwise is to tempt fate.

This much British guitar fan Tim Walker found out when he paid £1000 (about $1,600) for a guitar signed by Brian May, the guitarist from Queen (whose unique guitar sound comes in part from the use of a six-pence coin as a pick). Walker snapped up the guitar from a charity auction, and when it arrived, he was so thrilled with it that he couldn't resist rocking out with his new toy. When he was done, he discovered to his horror that his enthusiastic rockination had caused his sleeve to wipe off most of Brian May's signature. Now it just read "Bri," which was just enough of a signature for Tim to say to his friends "Look, that's Brian May's signature!" and for his friends to say "Yeah, *sure* it is, Tim," and roll their eyes.

There is a silver lining to this tale: Walker put in a call to Brian May's personal assistant, detailing his sad story; she took sympathy on the poor guy and passed along the tale to May, who agreed to resign the guitar. We hope that Tim will be more careful this time. Brian may not be so keen to sign again if another one bites the dust.

Source: *Daily Record* (UK), *The Sun* (UK)

THE CAMERA HAS STOPPED. PLEASE DON'T ACT ANYMORE

Daryl Hannah apparently has difficulty interacting with the press—and for good reason, if you've read most of the reviews of her acting (she was excellent in *Roxanne*, though. Check it out). So when the long-legged actress had to chat up the press at the premiere of *Kill Bill Volume 2*, in which she plays a ruthless one-eyed assassin named Elle Driver, she struck upon what she thought was a fine idea. Instead of talking to the press as Daryl, famous movie star, she'd chat them up as Elle, cold-blooded sword wielding killer: "So I went through the press line and I was standing on my car and doing kung fu and giving them the finger or whatever," she told a reporter for TeenHollywood.com.

How convincing was she? Convincing enough that when she later left the theater, there were policemen waiting for her, asking her to take a Breathalyzer test. Because, you see, in the real world, she's *not* Elle Driver, the hard-as-nails extinguisher of life—she's Daryl Hannah, actress. When celebrities seem memorably erratic at movie premieres, police tend to think they've probably got just a little too much of something alcoholic in their system.

Hannah had to talk to them to prove that she was sober (and sane) before they let her go about her life. "They couldn't seem to understand that I was just acting," she said. Well, Ms. Hannah, maybe they saw you in *Legal Eagles*.

Source: Ananova, TeenHollywood.com

A STEP DOWN FROM "CLAPTON IS GOD," TO BE SURE

If you ever want assurance that even the most famous of people on the globe aren't famous to everyone, everywhere, one need look no further than Eric Clapton, noted rock 'n' roll guitarist. From his early days with John Mayall, through Cream, Derek and the Dominoes, and his own solo work, Clapton has been consistently regarded as one of the most gifted—and famous—rock guitarists ever. But all that fame meant nothing in Surrey, England, when a cop pulled over Clapton's Ferrari for speeding.

According to news reports, the conversation between police officer Jim Jackson and one of the most popular and revered recording artists of the last half century went something like this:

Jackson: And what's your name, then?

Clapton: Eric Clapton, officer.

Jackson: So, Mr. Clapton, what do you do for a living to have such a nice car?

Clapton: I'm in the music business.

Jackson: Music business, eh? You must be doing okay, then.

And then he wrote Clapton a speeding ticket. It wasn't until later that Jackson's partner, a huge Clapton fan, got his pal up to speed on who it was he'd just pulled over. Or as the

UK paper *The Daily Record* put it, cheekily: "Jackson has since been debriefed about the identity of the little-known Ferrari driver. He can at least breathe a sigh of relief that a cranky Clapton did not shoot the sheriff."

Well, of *course* he didn't. Clearly Jackson was the deputy.

Source: *Daily Record* (UK)

TO TELL THE TRUTH

NBC's *The Apprentice* **was a huge hit when it aired.**
Viewers tuned in every week to watch teak-haired billionaire Donald Trump humiliate willing, would-be assistants.
After the first season had ended, the apprentice candidates
became mini-celebrities themselves, appearing on everything
from *Oprah* to *Larry King Live*. One particular contestant, a
woman by the name of Omarosa had become the one that
people loved to hate, mostly because she had developed quite
an evil reputation for lying that was clinched by the dramatic
season finale where cameras caught Ms. O spewing falsehoods
to her teammates. Omarosa defended herself vigorously on the
talk show circuit, despite all that the cameras had captured.

In one late-night appearance, when Omarosa was scheduled to appear on an April 2004 episode of the late night
Jimmy Kimmel Live show, she backed out of the appearance
midway through the taping. Just picked up and left, she did.
The reason—there was a lie detector on the set, and Omarosa
assumed it was for her. Apparently show producers had assured the jittery Omarosa that she wouldn't be strapped to
it—indeed, it was for a heavily promoted skit between host
Jimmy Kimmel and his Uncle Frank. Here's the thing: if you
become known for lying, there's a pretty good chance you
assume others aren't telling the truth either.

One assumes she left before her reputation could be
trashed by either refusing to submit to a lie detector test *or*
by failing a lie detector test. But rest assured Jimmy Kimmel
took care of that; after she ditched, Kimmel told the audience,
in the studio and over the air: "She left because the lie-

detector is out here. I'm not kidding, she was worried we were going to find out what a horrible, horrible, lying, filthy . . ." and then he trailed off while the studio audience laughed.

The moral? Don't lie, or at the very least, don't tell lies while there are rolling cameras trained on you. Or, at a minimum, don't cross Jimmy Kimmel on his own show.

Source: *New York Post*

A JEWEL OF A CONCERT

veryone agrees that the first show waifish folk-pop star
Jewel played at New Hampshire's Hampton Beach Ball-
room Casino in May 2004 was perfectly fabulous. But something happened between the first show and the second,
because when the blonde, snaggle-toothed songstress came
out for show number two she was apparently a bit unhinged.

Well, you say, she's a rock star. They're supposed to be
unhinged. Yeah, but it's supposed to be a *fun* sort of unhinged,
and this was, according to concertgoers, merely strange and
unpleasant. The singer began her set by mocking the fat and
the toothless (never a smart thing in a casino). Later, she
asked the crowd to yell requests and then told them to shut
up. To top it all off, Jewel eventually told the audience to stop
looking at her teeth (snaggly) and instead and look at her
breasts (not snaggly).

And then there was that ten-minute meandering discourse
on the antidepressants Zoloft and Paxil about halfway through
the show. As one concertgoer said to the *Hampton Union*
newspaper: "I don't know what that was all about. I don't
know if she was on it or what. Maybe she *didn't* take it."

In all, Jewel played four or five songs in an hour-long
concert, which is not very much. And for the encore? About a
minute's worth of yodeling. *That's* gonna drive t-shirt sales for
sure.

Source: The *Hampton Union*

SLAPPIN' TO THE OLDIES

Don't get **Richard Simmons angry.** You wouldn't *like* him when he's angry. No, the exercise guru *will* bring the slapdown. Don't think that just because he's, well, you know, Richard Simmons, that he won't mix it up. He is a man without *fear*.

Just ask Christopher Farney, who crossed paths with Mr. Simmons at Phoenix's Sky Harbor International Airport in March 2004. As a bit of background, let us note that Farney stood 6′2″, weighed 250 pounds, and worked as a motorcycle salesman and an ultimate cage fighter (a sport like wrestling but with less brains involved). This chunky hunk of a man saw the diminutive Mr. Simmons (5′7″, 155 pounds, 55 years old), who was waiting for his plane, and according to the police report, said "'Hey everybody. It's Richard Simmons. Let's drop our bags and rock to the '50s!'"

Well, rather than do the usual celebrity thing (which would be to smile mirthlessly at the lame joke, find out the name of the miscreant, and then have your minions ruin his credit record), Simmons walked over to Farney and said, "It's not nice to make fun of people with issues," and slapped the burly boy right across the kisser. Farney wasn't physically injured, but pressed misdemeanor assault charges against Simmons.

Does this mean Simmons is headed toward the big house? No, because Farney later dropped the charges in May.

Sources: TheSmokingGun.com, Associated Press, CBS News

The Really Stupid Quiz

BLAME IT ON THE FAME

Can you tell a true story from a fake one? One of these is true. Two of them could not be more fabricated if you found them in a tabloid. Which is which? Well, it's time to step into the spotlight and guess.

1. Shock rocker Alice Cooper has grown a softer side through his enthusiasm for playing golf. Every year, he sponsors a celebrity golf tournament, the proceeds of which go to Cooper's youth-oriented charity, the Solid Rock Foundation. But along with that enthusiasm comes a dark secret: a reputation on the fairways of his native Scottsdale, Arizona, for accidentally striking large numbers of course-residing animals with his drives. His most memorable incident occurred in 1998 when, while practicing for his tournament, Cooper knocked a goose right out of the sky, causing the guilt-stricken rocker to pay for the dazed animal's rehabilitation. "I feel terrible about it," Cooper said about his animal-striking reputation. "I really don't do it on purpose."

2. They say that the artist must suffer for the art; perhaps Oscar-winner Halle Berry had this in mind when she revealed on the Web site TeenHollywood.com that the preparation for her action film *Catwoman* gave her a serious and persistent case of flatulence: "It was wicked stuff," confessed one of the beautiful women in Hollywood. "I had

the worst gas in the world!" The proximate cause were protein shakes the actress drank to help bulk up. Something for you guys to remember. Coincidentally, we hear she's single now.

3. Pop star diva Christina Aguilera caused a ruckus at the Plaza Hotel in New York City when she pronounced the suite in which she was to be quartered as "utterly unacceptable" and demanded a new suite. The problem? The suite's Feng Shui was off, according to Aguilera's spokeswoman. "Christina is very sensitive to the energy flow of her surroundings," said the spokeswoman. "We had spoken to the Plaza staff beforehand, who assured us that the suite was in order." The Plaza Hotel management quickly moved Aguilera to another suite on the same floor and reportedly comped her stay for the egregious lack of *chi*.

Turn to page 329 for the answers.

The Annals of Ill-Advised Television

TODAY'S EPISODE: EMERIL

Welcome to the Annals of Ill-Advised Television, in which we look at some of the most inexplicably green-lit television shows in the history of the medium, and ask, "With shows this bad, how could the medium have possibly survived?" It's a stumper all right.

Starring in this Episode: Emeril Legasse and Robert Urich

Debut Episode: September 25, 2001, on NBC. Small bit of trivia: the show's debut was a week delayed because of 9/11 terrorist attacks.

The Pitch: Bam! It's America's favorite obnoxiously antic chef, Emeril! Bam! Chuckles abound as he plays himself, surrounded by lots of amusingly colorful characters who pretend to be involved in his real cooking show! Bam! And it has food! Bam! What could go wrong! BAM!

It Seemed Like a Good Idea at the Time Because: Emeril was a legitimate cultural phenomenon—a telegenic cook who made Cajun cooking accessible to Midwestern housewives, and whose popularity would pre-sell the show. The show would be produced, written, and directed by Harry Thomason and Linda Bloodworth-Thomason, who had created the hits

Designing Women and *Evening Shade,* so there was every expectation the show would hit the ground running.

In Reality: Well, it hit the ground, all right. Test audiences reportedly enjoyed the show's pilot, which featured Emeril at work and at home, but NBC executives hated it. The pilot had to be reshot and focused more on Emeril's cooking show and the side characters, which confused viewers since the show was ostensibly about Emeril himself, not his culinary pit crew. And Emeril himself didn't come off well: "The Food Network's most engaging frontman, Legasse, comes off stiffer than a well-whipped meringue when he has to play, um, himself," said E! Online. *The Detroit News* sent the show back to the kitchen, calling it "The worst sitcom of the year," and noting, "This could kill anyone's appetite."

How Long Did It Last? Ten episodes were filmed; just seven aired.

Were Those Responsible Punished? Neither Harry Thomason nor Linda Bloodworth-Thomason has done a series since, but Thomason has been busy with documentaries and a *Designing Women* reunion show. Emeril, of course, is still merrily Bam!-ing along on *Emeril Live* on the Food Network. It's as if everyone agreed to forget that whole crazy sitcom adventure ever happened.

CHAPTER 3

CHUG-A-LUG!

Heave you heard? Alcohol can make you do dumb things. We know—we were shocked when we heard, too. And yet, as story after story of intoxicated people acting dumb spilled on us like beer in the hands of a tipsy reveler, we had to admit that there was something to this "too much booze = big trouble" equation. Especially when there's some sort of vehicle involved, like, say, a bulldozer or a train.

And so we present the following stories strictly as a public service: laugh, drink and be merry—but be aware of the fine line where "merry" turns into dumb.

MMMMM...FELONIOUS BEER

The cellblock doors at the Hawkins County, Tennessee, jail were unlocked, and a faulty control panel meant that the jailers were none the wiser. The inmates, however, were only too aware of this fact. So one night, two of them made their move. They opened their cells, slipped out a fire exit, and then made a hole through the exercise yard fence to break free. So why did they come back shortly thereafter? Well, to hand out the beer, of course!

See, these inmates weren't interested in escaping—apparently they agreed with the social imperatives that required them to spend their time incarcerated. However, they didn't see why they couldn't knock back a brew just because they happened to be repaying their debt to society at the time. So our two inmates did not hightail it to parts unknown but rather to a local liquor store for a beer run. There, dressed in civilian clothes borrowed from other inmates (the jail didn't have enough orange jumpsuits to go around), they bought some beer and took it back to the big house. And when all the beer had been drunk, another two inmates went out to get some more. In all, the authorities believe the inmates consumed two cases of beer.

Naturally, the authorities were not pleased when they learned about the smuggled suds. They charged the four men for escaping and bringing alcohol into the jail. "I guess they thought if they came back they wouldn't be charged with escape," Sheriff Warren Rimer said, "but they were wrong." Yes, that'll teach 'em (unless the jail cells still aren't fixed).

Source: Associated Press

CHUG-A, CHUG-A, CHOO-CHOO!

As anyone who has overindulged knows, there's blacking out, and then there's *blacking out*. The first of these happens when you wake up the morning after a hard night of drinking at home, you're still in your clothes from the night before, and you have no idea how you wound up sleeping on the kitchen floor.

Somewhere past *that* is what happened to "Jorge," a hard-drinking Mexican citizen from the town of San Nicholas de los Garza. It seems that after a night of enthusiastic imbibing, Jorge lost track of, well, pretty much everything until he woke up with paramedics standing over his body, looking at him like he was some really interesting specimen of road kill.

Which in a way he was. The night before in a beer-hazed stupor, Jorge had apparently confused the local railroad tracks with his own bed. He snuggled down in between the rails for a long winter's nap. After he woke up, Jorge was shocked to learn what he had slept through: a train just plain running over him.

As it turns out, it's probably a good thing Jorge was so drunk because he did not move a muscle, which allowed the train to pass over his heavily slumbering body by a margin of just a few inches. If he had lifted his head at all, there's a good chance he would have lost it.

Once the paramedic roused Jorge from his little nap, he professed mystification as to how it all happened. "I counted only six beers," Jorge explained to local newspaper *El Norte*, although he then allowed "But who knows how many more there might have been. I don't remember." Yes, well. After the first six, they *do* tend to run together.

Source: Reuters

BULLDOZING BERLIN

One of the well-known side effects of alcohol is that funny effect it has on judgment: alcohol impairs it, and then (because alcohol is just that way), it doesn't do you the courtesy of letting you know that it's done so. So you *feel* as if you're making rational decisions when in *fact*, you're acting foolish.

Let's hope after an evening of beer-tinged fun you don't make the same judgments as "Rolf," a 28-year-old Berliner, who enjoyed too much of something in a Neukoelln district pub and then weaved out into the streets in the early hours of the morning. On his way to wherever he was going, Rolf passed by a bulldozer and found himself uncontrollably attracted to the machine. He climbed up in it, turned it on, and hit the road at about 20 miles per hour.

The Berlin cops saw the errant bulldozer and its drunken pilot. They ordered Rolf to pull over, but his impaired judgment helped him to ignore those silly little people with their silly little badges. Well, at least until they jumped on the bulldozer, broke the cab's window, and then spritzed him in the eyes with mace. Impaired judgment or not, chances are Rolf paid attention to blinding pain.

Rolf was arrested for drunk driving; there was also the small matter of the theft of the bulldozer. Rolf's next trip will be to the courthouse, where it's unlikely judgment will be impaired.

Source: Reuters

BLASPHEMY, AUSTRALIAN STYLE

We've heard nothing but good things about the Brazilians, a wonderful people who have a whole lotta fun during Carnivale, the Brazilians' take on Mardi Gras. However, the fine people of Brazil *do* have their limits, and if you test them, you'll be sorry.

An Australian, "Clive" discovered one of those limits during a vacation to Rio de Janerio. He and his mates visited the magnificent 100-foot statue of Jesus atop Corcovado Mountain, one of the city's top tourist attractions. Clive and a few of his buddies made a journey up the mountain not long after Carnivale had ended.

Clive was a bit intoxicated—not big news—and so were his pals. And so when they reached the statue, they thought it might be a lark if Clive took off his clothes and posed under the statue, holding his outstretched arms in an imitation of the statue itself. Clive, apparently an exhibitionist sort, didn't need much encouragement; he was out of his trousers in fairly quick order.

It was all good fun until an incensed Brazilian prosecutor, who just happened to be contemplating the statue at the same time, ordered the drunken lot of them arrested on the charge of committing an obscene act. The group was hustled off to a nearly police station, where they were held until they signed affidavits swearing that they would appear in court for their alleged crimes or they would never be allowed on Brazilian soil again.

Remember, if you act like a jerk, Jesus may forgive you, but the Brazilians may not.

Source: Reuters

FENCE FRUSTRATES
SLOSHED SWEDE

Sven's" first mistake was visiting the young woman—
or, should we say, *attempting* to visit the young woman.
Sven, a Swede who lived in Oslo, Norway, had a thing for a
Norwegian girl, and so he decided to make a social call on her.
Unfortunately for Sven, he was drunk and it was late at night.
The woman, not enthused about the appearance of an intoxicated Swede in her doorway, refused Sven entry. Well, Sven
might have been besotted in more ways than one, but he
wasn't a complete jerk. Rebuffed, he turned to go.

And was immediately beset by issues. The gate to the
young woman's apartment building had closed and locked,
and now he couldn't get back out to the street. This is the
point where a sober man might have sheepishly gone back and
asked the woman to buzz open the gate; but remember, Sven
wasn't sober. Having been tossed aside once that evening, he
was perhaps not looking for it to happen a second time. So he
attempted to slip under the gate. No dice.

Now did he go back and ask to be let out? Of course not.
Instead, he reasoned that his bulky clothes kept him from
sliding under the gate. And so, off came the clothes, and back
under the gate Sven went, only to get stuck. So now, we have
a rejected drunk, naked Swede pinned under a gate. And there
he stayed for several hours in the cold Norwegian night, contemplating love, the universe, and the night breezes on his
naked skin.

Eventually, passersby discovered Sven and called the police to extricate him. In the meantime, a team of ace reporters had gathered at the scene to document the event as it unfolded; Sven, crafty as he was, begged the gathered newsmen to say that he had gotten trapped while trying to save a kitten, a story that would have been compromised—nay, deeply *perverted*—by his undressed state. Sven later asked the reporters to note that the woman he'd come to visit was "a real stunner." It was indeed duly noted.

If this had happened in the United States, Sven probably would have been hauled into jail for public nudity, public drunkenness, and general gross stupidity. In Norway, they just told him to go home, take a shower, and sleep it off. So, if you're ever planning to get stuck naked under a gate, you know where to go.

Source: Associated Press

OH, IT WAS HAZARDOUS MATERIAL, ALL RIGHT

The Water Works employees of Erie, Pennsylvania, first believed something was up after they chased away a mysterious trespasser from the grounds of Sigsbee Reservoir, which contained 33 million gallons of water destined for the use of the good people of Erie. What on Earth would *anyone* be doing near a reservoir so early in the morning?

That's when they saw it: a black bag on the walkway that went around the reservoir. In this day and age, mysterious trespassers and even more mysterious black bags left at reservoirs are not to be trifled with. Fearing sabotage of the city water supply, the Water Works employees called the police. The police ordered a lockdown of the reservoir and of the surrounding neighborhood. Four hours later, members of the local bomb squad discovered that what was inside the black bag was definitely biological, and if not lethal, at least stinky: a pair of, shall we say, *aggressively used, soiled* underwear.

So how did it get there? Well, we're glad you asked. It seems that the night before, one "Terrance," an 18-year-old, partied a waaayyyy too hard—so hard, in fact, that he passed through the many stages of drunkeness. First there's drunk, then there's falling-down drunk, which can quickly turn into falling-down-and-puking-your-guts-out drunk. Then it starts to get even uglier when you progress to falling-down-and-puking-your-guts-out-with-no-bladder-control drunk, and finally there's one messy step beyond *that.*

Terrance went the extra mile to take that one step beyond, and as a result experienced a major party foul in his underwear. A sympathetic friend (who hopefully had a cold at the time) dragged him home, took him out of his violated attire, stuffed the dirty togs into the infamous black bag, and then hurled the bag over the fence onto the reservoir walkway. End of story.

Until the next morning, when Terrance remembered that the keys to his car were in his pants pocket. Whoops. Off Terrance went to retrieve the keys, only to be shooed away by the Water Works employee, who then found the bag and reported it. The local police and fire departments, the county emergency management team, the bomb squad, and the FBI were not at all thrilled to spend four hours of their life obsessing over what turned out to be a truly craptacular case.

Confronted by the police, Terrance admitted it was his underwear and eventually pled guilty to "defiant trespass," a misdemeanor. His punishment? A fine of $500 a month for ten months to pay for the cost of the emergency services. That should cut into his discretionary income for drinking. Terrence's remaining underwear is no doubt rejoicing at that bit of news.

Source: Associated Press, Erie *Times-News,* wjettv.com

BLESSED AREN'T THE DUMB

Ask yourself this question: if you were a man of the cloth, at what point in the following scenario would you plead for leniency from the police because of your special relationship with the Big Guy?

1. Sometime after you crashed your car but before police could evaluate you for intoxication;

2. After the cops began evaluating you for intoxication but before you punched one officer in the head when he wasn't looking;

3. After slugging one cop but before the other officer dropped you to the ground;

4. After hitting the ground but before the paramedics had to strap you to a gurney because you kept cursing and spitting at the police;

5. It really doesn't matter because after driving drunk, assaulting an officer, and resisting arrest, you could be Saint Paul and the cops would still be hauling your pious posterior into the pokey.

In the case of "Rod" it turns out that **5** was the correct answer. Early one June 2004 morning, Las Vegas police found Rod at the wheel of a car that had plowed into another vehicle; once the officers got Rod out of his car and started asking him questions, Rod decided it was in his best interest to punch one of the cops, because nothing says "I am sober" like blindsiding a member of the law enforcement community.

After this came the takedown, the cursing, the screaming, and the restraint by the EMTs.

Somewhere along the way, Rod mentioned his calling. "He was saying, 'I'm a Catholic priest! I'm a Catholic priest!'" said one officer who was at the scene, and indeed, Rod's license showed him dressed in a priest's collar. That's *Father* Drunken Verbally Abusive Cop-Hitter to *you,* pal. But just because you're a man of the cloth doesn't mean that the Big Guy and the cops are going to let you off the hook. Rod's blood alcohol count was 0.34, more than three times the limit.

"We're calling it the case of the holy spirits," said one police officer. Hey, now. You take down the drunks, pal. We'll handle the jokes.

Source: Las Vegas *Review-Journal*

THOSE WEREN'T THE SUDS
THEY WERE LOOKING FOR

Like most countries that don't actively promote alcoholism as a way of life, Sweden has strict laws about underage drinking. And like most countries where teenagers aren't chained to their parents 24–7, Swedish teens will find a way to get a buzz when they want to. Just how far they'd go, however, wasn't entirely clear until 2004's Baltic Sea Music Festival in Karlshamn.

The first signal promoters got that something was amiss was when a 14-year-old girl at the festival was briefly hospitalized with stomach pains. It turns out the teenager had taken liquid soap from the portable toilets at the festival and put it in her soda. Now while one readily admits that teenagers can do any range of stupid things for dubious reasons, this particular action seemed stranger than most. It was then someone remembered a relevant fact about that certain kind of soap—namely, that it was 62 percent alcohol.

This prompted officials from Bajamaja, the company from which the portable toilets had been rented, to check their latrines. "I suspected something was wrong because the soap went like hot cakes," said Anders Persson, of Bajamaja. Sure enough, the soap was gone—and by the end of the festival, many of the soap dispensers had been smashed. Those crazy kids. Who'd a thought you had to tell them not to drink soap?

Source: Associated Press

THE DRUNK NEED NOT APPLY

You want to be a state trooper in Washington State? Here's your first tip—apply only when sober.

"Paul" came into the State Patrol headquarters in Clark County, glassy-eyed and slurry-spoken, and asked for a job application. One of the troopers there suggested that asking for a job application from the police while intoxicated might not be such a great way to make a first impression.

Well, of course, Paul was indignant and denied this scandalous drinking rumor. Whereupon another trooper on the scene offered to give Paul a Breathalyzer test. Paul submitted and got a score of .095, comfortably above the .08 limit for legal intoxication. Oh, well, Paul said (or something like it), there was that Long Island Ice Tea he'd had; he quickly explained the fact that he hadn't eaten in more than a day might have been why the drink was hitting him so hard.

This was the part where the troopers asked Paul how he'd gotten to the headquarters. He claimed that someone drove him. "Uh-huh," they said, "Just remember not to drive home." Ten minutes later, troopers saw Paul get into a car and drive off. Let's just say the chase was not a particularly long one. He was given more tests, declared legally drunk, and ticketed. His sister had to come and get him.

"I guarantee he's not going to get a job with us," said Trooper Gavin March. "We've arrested drunks in unexpected ways and places before, but this one just blew me away." No doubt the citizens of Washington rest easier knowing Trooper Paul will not be on the case.

Source: Seattle *Times*

The Really Stupid Quiz

CHUG-A-LUG!

One is true. Two are false. You decide. Think of it as a sobriety test for your sense of reality.

1. Gibby's Bar and Grill in Tuscaloosa, Alabama, was doing a brisk business in its Green Machine Shooters—tangy, green-tinged vodka shots that Gibby's owner Thomas Garvey claimed featured a secret ingredient that he did not feel obliged to share. Then suspicious local authorities snuck out one of the shooters to a local lab for a chemical analysis, whereupon it was discovered that the secret ingredient was ethylene glycol—the primary ingredient in antifreeze, which in large enough doses can cause kidney failure, brain damage, and death. "He claimed that he thought he was using a brand that had propylene glycol, which is not as toxic," said a local law enforcement spokesman. "He didn't quite get that serving antifreeze of any sort is just not allowed."

2. Driving drunk will get you thrown in jail—but one computer whiz kid hopes that hacking while drunk will spare him the slammer. Albert Lee of New Haven, Connecticut, was arrested in May 2004 for authoring a variant of the "sobig" virus and sending it out on the e-mail systems of the world. Lee's lawyer said his client, a computer science major, intends to plea not guilty because he released the virus while he was drunk. "We're not disputing that he

coded the virus," said lawyer Jason Garcia. "But he did it as part of a class project on viruses. He would never have uploaded it if he hadn't have been in judgmentally impaired state of mind." Apparently, it was the booze pressing the "Send" button.

3. Not getting enough of a buzz from your booze? Perhaps you'd like to try a new drink produced in the Czech Republic—a flavored vodka where the added flavor attraction is not lemon, cherry, currant, or mint, but pot. Yes, it's marijuana-flavored vodka! Why the Czech citizenry would want to sample the alcoholic equivalent of bongwater isn't clear since they can't get stoned and drunk simultaneously from just drinking the beverage. There is no tetrahydrocannabinol (better known as THC, the active ingredient in marijuana) in the vodka. The potable is actually made from hemp, pot's industrial sibling with a very low THC content. So if you get the munchies after a couple of shots, chances are you're just drunk and hungry.

Turn to page 329 for the answer.

Dim Bulbs in Bright Lights
THiS iS SPiNAL TAP (1984)

Our Dumb Guys: Nigel Tufnel (Christopher Guest), David St. Hubbins (Michael McKean), and Derek Smalls (Harry Shearer), collectively the core of the heavy metal group Spinal Tap

Our Story: Metal group Spinal Tap's 1982 North American tour becomes progressively more chaotic as the band's album release is pushed back, concert dates are canceled, and band members get on each others' nerves. Interspersed with the road drama are individual and group interviews with the members, in which it becomes apparent that the rock and roll life style is not good for the brain cells.

Dumb or Stoned? Well, stoned is a given when dealing with heavy metal rock "gods" from 1982 (at one stressful point, David St. Hubbins allows that he might be more upset if he weren't in fact so heavily sedated). The real question is, are these guys dumb because they're stoned, or were they that way naturally?

High Point of Low Comedy: The performance of the song "Stonehenge," in which a foot-high model of the famous mighty rock monument is in clear and present danger of being trampled by dancing dwarves.

And Now, In Their Own Words: David St. Hubbins's deep response when asked if the Spinal Tap was near the end: "Well, I don't really think that the end can be assessed as of itself as being the end because what does the end feel like? It's like saying when you try to extrapolate the end of the universe, you say, if the universe is indeed infinite, then how—what does that mean? How far is all the way, and then if it stops, what's stopping it, and what's behind what's stopping it? So, what's the end, you know, is my question to you."

They're Dumb, But Is the Film Good? It *rocks*. Even though it's not the first "mockumentary" ever (as anyone who's ever seen *The Rutles* will tell you), it's certainly the best since it is the one to which all others are compared. Even real documentaries are compared to it—when Metallica released its 2004 documentary *Some Kind of Monster* (in which the band members enter group therapy), the single most frequent comparison that film had in reviews was to *Spinal Tap*.

CHAPTER 4

DUMBING IN THE FAMILY

No matter what side of the "Nature vs. Nurture" debate you fall on, it's pretty easy to see that families can be a source of dumbness. Well, it makes sense, doesn't it? After all, who do people spend most of their time with? That's right, their families.

In a way it's reassuring. The old saying is that "a family that plays together, stays together." Families that act stupid together also stay together, and often in the same holding pen. *That's* family dumbness for you!

SO HAPPY TOGETHER...

Here's the first thing: of all the people to attempt a citizen's arrest upon, an actual sheriff's deputy is not one of them. "Adam," a citizen of McMinnville, Tennessee, nevertheless attempted to arrest off-duty Deputy Lt. Stan Hillis for speeding. After pulling up behind Lt. Hillis's parked civilian car, one thing inevitably led to another and it was *Adam* who was arrested, for disorderly conduct, resisting arrest, and evading arrest. In one of those interesting twists, this all went down right across from the local jail, so the deputy and Adam didn't have far to go.

Adam's one phone call went to his mom, "Abby," who drove to the jail with 17-year-old son "Bret" in tow. Once they had arrived, Bret allegedly decided that it might be a fine idea to slap one of the deputies. And now, words of wisdom from Sheriff Jackie Matheny: "If you strike an officer, you're going to jail 100 percent of the time." And of course, Bret was conveniently and already there—another transportation problem easily solved.

Then Abby got in on the act. Having both her cubs in the slammer aroused Abby's mother bear instincts. She allegedly became very loud and refused to obey the orders of law enforcement officials, otherwise known as disorderly conduct and resisting arrest. Mama bear got caged, too.

So who was left in this family menagerie? Why, "Al," the family patriarch. He showed up and also allegedly became very disorderly and uncooperative, so much so that out came the tasers—*zap!*—and now you had the entire family cooling its heels behind bars. That's where they stayed for the next three hours before they made bail.

When family therapists say families should spend more time doing things together, this really *isn't* what they mean. Try Yahtzee instead. And don't attempt any citizen's arrests while playing.

Source: wkrn.com, Associated Press, newschannel5.com

THEY'RE ALWAYS IN THE LAST PLACE YOU LOOK

We're the last people in the world to say that when it looks like one of your kids is missing, you shouldn't ask for (and receive) a full-blown search and rescue party. There isn't a parent alive who doesn't live in fear of their kid just disappearing, and then facing gut-gnawing anxiety until the child is found safe and unharmed. So, please, if the kid has gone missing, call out the cops. And the dogs. And the neighbors. And the psychics. But please, before you do all that, you might want to check behind the sofa first.

"Ann," of Morecambe, Lancashire, England, had lost track of her three-year-old right round teatime (that's late afternoon, for the Yanks); she assumed that her sister, who had gone across the street with her seven-year-old, had also brought the younger child with her. But when Ann went to retrieve her children, the youngest was nowhere to be found. Naturally, Ann was concerned (well, frantic, actually) and called the police.

Thereupon commenced an admirable flurry of activity from the local constabulary and the neighborhood residents. They even called in a helicopter to hover over the area and to broadcast a description of the little girl. For three hours police and neighbors searched to no avail. And then, someone had the bright idea to look behind Ann's couch. There was the sleeping three-year-old wrapped in a blanket. What was the kid doing, sleeping behind a couch? Well, you know kids. They're always doing something weird. And apparently the kid was a deep sleeper: "My house was swarming with police and [she] didn't wake up once," Ann told reporters.

Total cost of the search-and-rescue? About $50,000. "I was so relieved she was safe and well but did feel bad about that," Ann said, of the cost of the baby-finding mission. Let's hope they don't send her the bill, or that three-year-old might be out of a college education.

Source: Scotsman.com, *The Sun* (UK), *Morecambe Today* (UK)

BUT YOU CAN GET THE LITHOGRAPH FOR JUST $25K!

If you've ever put a preschool picture by one of your kids on the fridge, you know while you might believe the picture is priceless, a genuine art appraiser might—and no offense to your kid—beg to disagree (unless by "priceless," you meant to imply "worthless"). With that in mind, come along down under, to Australia, and to an "art auction" at the ritzy St. Catherine's school, in Toorak, Melbourne.

The "artwork" in question: a large, colorful painting done by members of the preschool class at St. Catherine's—lots of animals and people in typically preschool representations. It wasn't a Picasso, in other words (unless Pablo was having a terrible day). But millionaire John Ilhan's young daughter wanted it, or so he said in an interview with the *Herald Sun* newspaper, so he made an offer for it.

And that's when another parent stepped in and (as Ilhan tells it) informed him that she had deeper pockets than he. And then to prove it, she raised the bid on the painting. Well, apparently Ilhan was not the sort of man who made millions—even in Australian dollars—by turning down a challenge. So he and the woman promptly started a bidding war until finally Ilhan decided that thing had "got seriously out of hand."

The final bid? It was $75,000 in Australian dollars (about $53,000 U.S.), and Ilhan's nemesis got the painting. That chunk of change would be enough to buy art from actual Australian artists—famous and *good* ones, even. But you know how excited people get when they have more competitive spirit (and money) than sense.

Interestingly, the bidding war actually seems to have been more about the getting than the having, since the winning bidder eventually returned the artwork to the school. It seems unlikely that the artwork would ever sell for that much again. But then again, maybe it will. Now it's famous, and there are always collectors who are willing to one-up someone else. Let's hope the fame doesn't go to the young artists' heads. In the meantime, maybe you'll want to get that refrigerator art appraised after all.

Source: *Herald Sun* (Australia)

LONG-TERM STORAGE?

There are many different types of burial practices in the world, performed by all the various cultures that exist on this globe of ours. There are mausoleums, graves, cremations, funeral pyres, burials at sea, and even the option of leaving your body to science so medical students can get more familiar with your internal organs than you ever were. All of them are beautiful in their own way, except maybe that one with the medical students, but even *that* has some instructional value. But as far as we know, *no* culture advises sticking your father's corpse in an air-conditioned storage locker for three months.

And yet, that's what "Len" did after his father passed on (from natural causes) in a motel in Osceola County, Florida, in March 2004. To be fair to Len, even *he* knew that jamming dad into a storage locker wasn't the right thing to do. But Len was in a bind: he'd heard that funerals are expensive these days (and they are: the average one goes for about six grand), and he didn't have that kind of cash lying around. But he *did* have the $68.48 a month for a 5-by-10-foot storage locker. So, after wrapping up pop in a drop cloth and a garbage bag and telling his mom that he was taking her deceased spouse to a funeral home, he slipped his father into the locker. For three months.

We realize you're probably not a forensic scientist or anything, but take an educated guess here: what do *you* think happens to a human body after three months in a storage locker? If you guessed "I'm pretty sure it would start to smell—really *bad*," you're ready for a guest shot on *CSI Miami*. Indeed, dad's decomposing body started to smell—really bad. The managers of the storage facility (who did not know what was in the storage locker) kept calling Len to tell him he needed to check his storage space because it smelled like something died in there. Perhaps, they were thinking maybe just a rodent.

Realizing he couldn't keep dad in storage for much longer, Len made a decision. To come clean and properly bury dad? Well, no. His next step was to transfer dad from the storage locker to a rented U-Haul truck ("Adventures in Moving" indeed!) and then park that truck in front of his own house. Len failed to appreciate that a body that smells bad in an air-conditioned storage locker doesn't smell any better in the back of a U-Haul baking in the sun. Soon the neighbors started complaining about the smell. After confiding in a friend, Len eventually came clean to the authorities and cut a deal with them to properly put his poor dad to rest.

It turns out that if you can't afford to bury someone, generally speaking your local authorities can help you find a way to do it, since it's not a good idea to leave bodies lying around—stuffed in storage lockers or otherwise. Give it some thought before you have to lie to the storage facility manager about what you're keeping in that space you're renting.

Source: Local10.com, wftv.com, *Orlando Sentinel*

DOES THE DUFFEL BAG
COST EXTRA?

We've got a personality test for you. You're at the beach, when a guy comes up to you with an infant in a duffel bag and asks you if you'd be interested in buying. Do you:

1. Haggle on a price;

2. Smile weakly at the guy's clearly lame sense of humor and walk away briskly; or

3. Call the cops on the sick loser?

No, no, you don't really have to answer; we know all of you picked **3** (*right?*). And the reason for this is pretty obvious: sure, it's funny when Monty Python sells off a passel of children for medical experiments in *The Meaning of Life,* but in the real world, the idea of jocularly suggesting to strangers that you'd be willing to part with your baby, who you keep in a duffel bag, is creepy and wrong. *Everybody* know this.

Well, almost everyone. Then there's "Joe," a young Pennsylvania father. Joe and his wife were at the beach in Wildwood Crest, New Jersey, with their four-month-old son, when the wind whipped up and started blowing sand around. To protect their child from the elements, the couple advisedly placed their infant in an open duffel bag. And that's when Joe got the "bright" idea of walking up to total strangers, showing them the incongruous sight of a baby in a bag, and asking them if they'd like to buy the baby. What yuks!

Yes, a good time was had by all, or at least by one, until the police showed up, charged Joe and his wife with child endangerment, and briefly put the baby in the care of Child Protective Services. It seems that approaching random strangers and telling them that you're interested in unloading your baby to them makes people call the police to tell them all about you because they *believe* you. They have no idea you're just some idiot with a really bad sense of humor. They don't know you at all. That's why they're *called* "strangers."

After a nice long conversation with Joe and his wife, the local police were eventually convinced that they didn't actually have baby-sellers on their hands, just people with a maladjusted sense of what's funny. "Right now we're leaning toward a conclusion that it was not an authentic offer," a police spokesman told *The Philadelphia Inquirer*. "But if he thought he was being funny, it sure wasn't very humorous." Well, it's kind of funny *now*. Just not in the way Joe intended.

Source: *The Philadelphia Inquirer,* Associated Press, ABC News

SOMEONE LEFT THE RAKE
OUT IN THE RAIN

Timmy," **who was twelve,** was misbehaving in school. So
naturally Timmy's mom knew that she had to discipline
her child to make him understand the consequences of his
actions. And of course, that's fine: the parent who won't discipline his or her own child creates a problem child for the rest
of us.

Timmy's mom's choice of discipline: Timmy had to rake
the leaves in the front yard! Well, that's tough but fair; it's
physical labor and something most kids don't enjoy, but at the
same time it's something useful, and at least the boy will get
some fresh air. So, on balance, a reasonable punishment. Get
raking, Timmy!

Oh yeah, one other thing, said Timmy's mom. Timmy
would be raking the leaves completely naked. In the rain. With
high winds. While the temperatures are in the 40s.

And it's here, alas, that Timmy's mom lost us. And apparently, she lost the rest of the neighbors in her Virginia neighborhood, too, since one of them called the police to complain
that a twelve-year-old was out naked in the rain. Timmy was
still in the front yard, rake in hand, when the cops rolled up.
Shortly thereafter they rolled away with Timmy's mom in tow
because she'd been charged with felony child neglect, which,
speaking of appropriate discipline, can get you five years in the
Virginia pen.

Source: *Freelance-Star* (Fredricksburg, VA)

The Really Stupid Quiz

DUMBING IN THE FAMILY

One of the stories below has good relations with the truth. Two of them are shady second cousins. Which is which? That's for us to know and you to guess.

1. The "evil twin" concept, beloved by Hollywood, got a real life workout when Tim Garrity of Dallas, Texas, was cited for disturbing the peace when witnesses saw his truck and a man matching his description tearing up and down residential streets in the early morning hours. But Garrity was home sleeping next to his wife at the time of the events. However, Garrity's identical twin brother, Charlie, who lived with their parents less than a mile away, had keys to both Tim's house and his truck. Upon questioning, Charlie initially denied borrowing the car, but admitted to a drunken joyride after persuasion from his mother, who, as Dallas police officer Wayne McDonald said, "smacked him upside the head and told him to tell the truth."

2. Kids sure love their video games, but some kids like their video games more than others. A lot more. Like, to a dangerously unhealthy degree. Like "Soo," a Hong Kong thirteen-year-old so wrapped up in his computer game that he hardly noticed when midnight rolled around. His dad noticed the time and came in to tell Soo to give it a rest. Well, Soo didn't want to give it a rest, so dad did that parental thing dads do, and went over to the wall socket

and unplugged the computer. And then Soo did that thing kids do when dads do the parental thing, which was to go into the kitchen, grab a knife, and go after his father with it. Oh, wait, that's not actually what most kids do. Silly us. Well, dad managed to overpower Soo, the police were called and no one ended up getting hurt. But we suspect that's it for video games for Soo. And rightly so.

3. Aaah . . . the miracle of birth! Typically, it's a typical time for celebratation but an atypical time to get arrested. That's what happened in St. Louis, Missouri, when several relatives of a delivering woman were arrested at St. John's Mercy Medical Center. The mother-to-be had requested that several family members be allowed to observe the birth; the request was initially granted, but "The family members would keep getting in the way," said nurse Juanita Ocampo, who assisted the doctors. "They were all really casual about it, like they were at a cookout, not a birth." The doctor eventually asked the room to be cleared of everyone except the woman's husband, but the relatives, feeling insulted, became hostile. How dare the doctor try to remove distractions from the baby's delivery? Of all the nerve! The doc then paged hospital security, who called in the police who escorted the relatives out of the delivery room, so the doctor, could like do his job and stuff.

Turn to page 329 for the answer.

The Annals of Ill-Advised Television

TODAY'S EPISODE: THE SECRET DIARY OF DESMOND PFEIFFER

Starring in this Episode: Chi McBride and Dann Florek

Debut Episode: October 5, 1998, on UPN

The Pitch: Desmond Pfeiffer (the "p" is pronounced, and played by McBride) is a black, British gentleman in the 1860s who is exiled from Britain for cheating at cards. Desmond moves to the U.S. and finds employment as a butler in the White House of Abraham Lincoln (Florek). Think of it as *Benson,* only during the Civil War.

It Seemed Like a Good Idea at the Time Because: UPN, with its tiny viewership, was carving out a niche with "urban" comedies, and this seemed up their alley. Plus show creators Barry Fanaro and Mort Nathan had won Emmys for writing and producing *The Golden Girls.*

In Reality: The NAACP got whiff of the idea that *Desmond* would be deriving yuks from slavery and called for a boycott of the show, which pretty much stripped the show of any "urban" credibility it might have. UPN, somewhat panicked, pulled the pilot episode and started the series with another episode instead. Not that it mattered, as television critic Philip Michaels commented on Teevee.org: "No, *Desmond Pfeiffer* isn't racist. It is, however, unspeakably lame." Another misstep was to portray Abe Lincoln as a sex-starved, dim-bulb who engaged in "telegraph sex" with strange women; one could argue that, in theory, the show was satirizing the events of the Clinton White House, but it would be a pretty weak argument.

How Long Did It Last? Four episodes, with the final episode airing October 26, 1998. Nine episodes were completed; five, including the pilot, never aired.

Were Those Responsible Punished? Some. *Desmond* creators Fanaro and Nathan went on separately to make bad movies: Fanaro wrote the senior-citizen crime caper flop *The Crew* while Nathan wrote and directed the punishingly awful flop *Boat Trip*. McBride went on to act in a better TV series (*Boston Public*) and was most recently in the summer movies *The Terminal* and *I, Robot*. Dann Florek retreated back in the *Law and Order* universe that had made him famous; he plays a captain on *Law & Order: Special Victims Unit*.

CHAPTER 5

EDU-MA-CATioN

"Teach your children well," says the song. Well, that's not what happened in this chapter; in this chapter, we've got people teaching children very, very poorly. Although to be fair, the kids do their part as well. But hey! They're kids. They have an excuse. The adults in this chapter, on the other hand, we have to wonder about. How did they get out of high school? (We have some theories, but they're not very nice.)

THE CLASS ENDED WITH A BANG

In Orlando, Florida, there's this great program for kids called, "The Game of Life, The Game of Golf," that aims to introduce underprivileged youngsters to the sport. But an additional part of the class involves teaching kids to make smart life choices—like, for instance, being careful around loaded weapons.

Enter "Agent Smith," from the Drug Enforcement Agency (better known to us as the DEA) and his .40 caliber duty weapon. During the class, Agent Smith took out the gun, removed the magazine, and then pulled back the slide to clear the chamber—indeed, he had one member of the audience of about fifty adults and children come up and confirm that there was no bullet in the chamber.

As a brief interruption, we'd like to say that we don't know much about handguns and the handling thereof, but we do know not to ever, *ever* take anyone else's word on whether a gun is loaded or not. They could be lying, they could be idiots, or they could miss that one last little bullet. Treating every gun as if it's loaded is the smart way to go. Now, back to the action.

Once the audience member confirmed there was no bullet in the gun, Smith released the slide—which caused the bullet in the "unloaded" gun (surprise!) to blast out of the barrel and imbed itself in Agent Smith's thigh (it was only a flesh wound). A spectator who brought her nephew to the class related to the *Orlando Sentinel:* "My first thought was that it was part of his presentation. I thought it was a blank and he was trying to make a point about how easy it is to fire, to get the kids' attention. But then I looked at the agent's face and he looked surprised."

The good news is that Agent Smith's pain was not in vain since he did get through to those kids about the dangers of loaded weapons, just not in the way he had originally planned. The spectator also noted, "The point of gun safety hit home . . . after seeing that, my nephew doesn't want to have anything to do with guns." We suspect Agent Smith doesn't either.

Source: *Orlando Sentinel, The Washington Times*

DEATH BY PEANUT BUTTER!

There's nothing funny about nut allergies. But in the *particular,* there's not a thing amusing about someone having an allergic reaction so instantaneous and severe that their breathing passages constrict, anaphylactic shock sets in, and only a fast jab of adrenaline keeps someone on this side on the Styx (the mythological river, not the band).

This may be why the South Orange school district in New Jersey suspended a sixth grader for three weeks after the student allegedly threatened a teacher with . . . a package of Nutter Butter cookies. It seems that the teacher had a severe nut allergy, and the student in question had an unopened pack of said cookies in class *and* had made some untoward suggestions to other classmates regarding the application of said cookies to said teacher.

For discussing assault with a deadly cookie, you can get suspended these days? Yeesh. We can see how an actual attempt to rub said cookies on the teacher would certainly have been a problem. Hard time for the kid and a refusal of admittance to all the Ivy League schools (well, except maybe Brown) would have been an appropriate punishment. Better yet, if he dove across the cafeteria, peanut butter cookie in one hand, a small bust of noted peanut scientist George Washington Carver in the other, he'd still win points for creativity, but still meet with a suspension, too. But suspending a kid for just talking about the Nutter Butter's capabilities as a weapon? That's harsh, man. (We can remember some of the comments we made about our teachers. We'd be looking at jail time nowadays.)

This is also a reminder to teachers out there: telling a class of middle school kids about potentially fatal allergies you have is like giving yourself a nasty paper cut and then swimming in the shark pool—not a good idea. If you're going to tell them you're allergic to something, tell them you're allergic to BMWs. Or Brad Pitt. Let's see the kids smuggle one of those into class in their backpacks.

Source: Associated Press

TO THE SHOWERS, COACH

What do we want, hope, and expect from a middle school basketball coach? Optimally, we'd hope for one of those coaches who can take a collection of raggedy kids and diligently craft them into a team of players that trusts each other as they take to the hard court—and take on life. Realistically, we'll settle for anyone who makes sure the players shoot into the right basket at least 80 percent of the time.

"Chad" who coached basketball for a Pleasantville, New Jersey, middle school, appeared to lack proper motivational skills. For some reason, Chad believed that public humiliation is what makes the junior high athlete great. The evidence for this came when Chad presented one of his players with a very special award at the annual team banquet. Was it for most team spirit? Best bench warming? Most pronounced ability to draw the foul?

Nope, it was an award for the biggest crybaby on the team. Presenting a trophy with a crying baby on it to the thirteen-year-old recipient, Chad recounted how the boy "begged to get in the game, and all he did was whine." To add insult to injury, the boy's name was misspelled on the trophy.

Chad would later maintain the award was a joke. But oddly enough, the school board had difficulty in finding the nugget of humor in that particular act, and voted to keep Chad from ever coaching again in Pleasantville. In addition, he had to publicly apologize to the student and take sensitivity training classes. That's a start.

Sources: Associated Press

IT TASTED JUST LIKE STUPIDITY

Yes, we know. All fizzy things look so *tasty.* But tell that to "Tim," a junior from Odessa, Texas, who was presented with a flask of something from the chemistry lab by his alleged friends and bet $2 that he wouldn't drink from it. Well, two bucks is two bucks, and a bet's a bet, right? Tim thought so and took a swig. Was it refreshing? Yes, if you define "refreshing" as "causing one to bleed from the nose and mouth," which was how Tim was found later in the school's hallway. Alas, he did not have a Coke and a smile.

What was it he drank? They weren't sure. "We need to find out what it was from the toxicologist," assistant principal Ray Lascano told the local press. "All of those materials belonged to one of the chemistry labs." And generally what's kept in a chemistry class are chemicals, most of which are not meant to be ingested. You want to ingest chemicals, go down the hall to the cafeteria. Those chemicals, at least, aren't likely to make you bleed from the mouth. (Unless it's the tacos; watch out, those tortillas can be pointy.)

Tim didn't die, but he spent time in a pediatric intensive care unit before he got sent home. Hopefully with the $2 he won he can afford to buy himself a clue. Or at least some friends who won't try to slip him toxic fizz.

Sources: Associated Press

NOT WHAT THEY
MEANT BY SEX ED

Akio," an unassuming fellow from Tondabayashi, Osaka
Prefecture, Japan, just wanted to watch some adult entertainment, but didn't want his family to know about it. So
there he was, with the XXX title he had rented from the local
video store and no place to watch it. But then Akio had an
idea. There was a video player at his place of employment—
he could just watch it there! What a great idea.

Two problems. First of all, Akio's place of employment
was a junior high school where he was a teacher. Most work
places frown on employees using office equipment to indulge
themselves, but watching that kind of film in a place where
twelve-year-olds come to learn is a big ol' no-no. But perhaps
Akio was under the impression that if he were careful, then he
wouldn't have a problem. Like must dummies, he thought he
wouldn't get caught.

Second problem: the thing about pornography is that it
does tend to cloud one's judgment, as it did with Akio. After he
had snuck in a few minutes of his adult video in the science
room of his school, he left the room—and the tape in the
VCR, where it was discovered a few minutes later when a class
filed in to use the science room and also the video player. We
don't know what the class was expecting to learn that day,
but what they got was a few minutes of explicit sex education.
Akio got slapped with a one-month pay cut. Wonder how he'll
explain *that* at home.

Source: *Daily News* (Mainichi, Japan)

EVEREST IS NOT iN THE CARDS

One of the problems people have with nature is that they
simply don't *get* that nature is just itchin' to kill them at
the first opportunity. Nature is a famously cruel and unforgiv-
ing instructor, something the schoolteachers and students in
this story failed to appreciate.

On that note, we're on our way to Scotland, to Meall a'
Bhuachaille, a 2,500-foot hill north of Loch Morlich, in the
Cairngorms National Park. "Meall a' Bhuachaille" means
"Shepherd's Hill," which sounds pleasant enough, and it's not
like 2,500 feet seems very high, right? But as the members of
the Cairngorm Mountain Rescue Team will be happy to tell
you, get lost and alone on Shepherd's Hill, and you're just a
good storm away from being a hikersicle. That's why you take
proper hiking clothing, some provisions, a compass, and ways
to signal for help.

None of which the hiking party from the Beth Jacob
Teachers' Training Seminary in east London bothered with
before they set out to hike the hill in early July 2004. The
hiking party consisted of nearly forty 16- and 17-year-old girls
led by a single teacher; the girls' attire consisted of their
school uniform and sneakers, and the teacher led them without so much as map.

So naturally, the mist rolled in (in July? Believe it—there
had been snow on the summit of the hill until mid-June, and
a week before the temperature on the summit had gone well
below freezing), and the hiking party became irretrievably
lost. Not to mention the cold—some of the girls took to wrap-
ping themselves in trash bags for warmth. As one rescuer later

put it, they were "only a rain shower away from death," which is the last place you expect to be on a July afternoon.

The teacher eventually did find a way to signal for help—by borrowing a cell phone from one of her students to dial 999 (the UK equivalent of 911). Even then, the members of the Cairngorm Mountain Rescue Team had a difficult time locating the hiking group because of the mist, bad cell connections, and of course, the group's having no idea where they were. When the rescue team finally *did* locate them, the girls in the group were (can you believe it?) rather snippy: "What took you so long? We called for help 45 minutes ago," one of them reportedly said.

John Allen, who led the Rescue Team, was so appalled at the situation that he went on record to the press to commemorate the group's dumbassery: "I have never seen so many people so ill-equipped," he said to reporters. "Neither the teacher nor the girls had any idea of what they were doing or how much danger they were in. I hate to criticize people who enjoy hill walking and I very rarely do it, but this was probably the worst case I have ever encountered and I hope that by condemning the school and the teacher something useful will come out of it."

By all indications, however, it probably won't. "We were a bit worried lost in the mist, but it cleared up. I don't see what the fuss is all about," said one of the girls, after she had gotten down off the mountain. Well, take her back up the mountain, we say. She'll figure out what the fuss was about soon enough. Nature will take care of *that*.

Source: Scotsman.com, *The Daily Record* (UK), *The Telegraph* (UK)

The Really Stupid Quiz
EDU-MA-CATION

Time for a pop quiz! One story here is true. Two stories are false. Pick the true one and you get an "A." Pick a false one and you stay after class to beat the erasers. And remember, no looking at anyone else's answers.

1. A Red Bluff, California, biology teacher was placed on leave after he encouraged his biology students to name their frogs after the high school principal and other faculty members before they began their dissections. "As he handed out the frogs, he said it would help us get out our aggressions by pretending they were teachers we didn't like," one student said, "It was really creepy." Some students told their parents, who informed principal Patrick Gleeson. Sources at the Red Bluff Union School District offices suggest the incident occurred after another teacher had parked in the biology teacher's favorite parking space.

2. Every kid wants to drive the school bus. However, every kid should not be *allowed* to drive the school bus, particularly when the kids in question are aged eleven to fifteen. The good news is that the Carroll, Iowa, school bus driver did not, in fact, let all the kids on the bus drive the bus. The bad news is that six of the kids *did* get into the driver's seat for a bit of highly illegal, definitely dangerous, real-life Tonka time. Oddly enough, this caused the bus driver to hand in a resignation letter three weeks later. So now

Carroll, Iowa, is down one bus driver. On the other hand, they have at least six new candidates to take over the route.

3. Teachers at Taos Middle School in New Mexico experienced an ironic episode of embarrassment when the video at the heart of a voluntary sex education assembly was interrupted by several spliced-in scenes of *The Teletubbies,* the British children's show that features a quartet of colorful sprites. According to witnesses, the video was just starting a section on the changes bodies undergo during puberty when the spliced children's characters popped up and began their usual scampering and giggling. This undoubtedly broke the mood for the twelve-year-olds in the assembly. School officials suspect the dubbing was done when someone took the tape from the school districts main administrative offices and promised an investigation.

Turn to page 329 for the answer.

Dim Bulbs in Bright Lights

FAST TIMES AT RIDGEMONT HIGH (1982)

Our Dumb Guy: Jeff Spicoli (Sean Penn)

Our Story: The entire film is a slightly fictionalized account of a year at a California high school, written by journalist Cameron Crowe (who actually posed as a student to get the scoop on high school life). The Spicoli character's subplot features his ongoing struggle against the officious history teacher Mr. Hand (Ray Walston), who appears to delight in harshing the laid-back Spicoli's mellow buzz.

Dumb or Stoned? Since one of the first appearances of Jeff Spicoli features him stumbling out of a VW van packed with more herb smoke than a Jackson Browne concert, we can pretty much say he was stoned.

High Point of Low Comedy: Spicoli orders pizza to be delivered during history class and is totally shocked when Mr. Hand parcels out the pizza to other kids in the class—and then totally has a slice himself!

And Now, In Their Own Words: Spicoli, explaining the reasoning behind the U.S. Constitution to Mr. Hand: "So what

Jefferson was saying was 'Hey! You know, we left this England place because it was bogus. So if we don't get some cool rules ourselves, pronto, we'll just be bogus too.' Yeah?"

He's Dumb, But Is the Film Good? It's very good, and is still one of the most observant teen films ever made. In many ways, *Fast Times* is the blueprint for just about every other teen movie of the 1980s.

CHAPTER 6

GOVERNMENT GOOFS

We know, we know: chronicling governmental goofs is like shooting fish in a barrel. But it's a barrel you paid for. You paid for the fish, too. So, you know, someone ought to have the fun of shooting. Why not us? Not that we're actually advocating shooting at the government. That would be wrong. (Please governments, don't lock us up. We're merely being metaphorical, here.) So do your civic duty and read on to see just what those tax dollars are paying for.

UNCLE SAM CHARGES IT

What happens when you give a U.S. federal civil servant a charge card? Most of the time, they use it for what it's supposed to be used for: gas for cars on government business, staples, a computer monitor or two for the office. You know. The usual.

But of course, not everyone plays nice with their government-supplied credit cards, paid off with your tax dollars (presuming you're an American taxpayer). In a 2004 audit of government credit card use, here are some of the credit card doozies the GAO uncovered:

- A navy employee spent more than $130,000 on cars, a motorbike, and breast implants. Yes, the credit card spending went to her head, but your tax dollars went to her chest.

- An employee at the Department of Defense ran a little scam with a family member to make fake purchases through a sham company. They caught her only after $1.7 million in purchases went through. That's government efficiency for you!

- After being asked to explain the purchase of a stuffed deer head, one credit card holder explained it was to teach military personnel about the local animal life.

- Another justified the purchase of a trio of global positioning systems because the cardholder just kept getting lost.

- How are navy engineers learning about robotics? To hear one card holder explain it, through the purchase of a couple hundred dollars worth of Lego toys.

- And finally, some credit for not insulting the intelligence of the auditor: when one government card holder was asked to explain why there was a need to buy a $250 day planner from designer Louis Vuitton instead on one you can pick up for $12 at Staples, the card holder responded: "Personal preference." Well, you know. When someone else is buying, that'd be *our* personal preference, too.

Now when you think of the U.S. government's $7 trillion deficit, you'll have to stay up nights wondering how much of it is being charged at the average credit card APR of 18.9 percent. Sweet dreams!

Source: Reuters

CYPRUS? IT'S NEAR CRETE. REALLY NEAR.

You would think that the average Irish citizen would be aware of where the island of Cyprus is in the Mediterranean Sea: Cyprus is a small island split into two states (The Republic of Cyprus and the Turkish Republic of Northern Cyprus) that don't really get along—which *is* something the Irish can certainly understand, come to think of it.

You would also think that the Irish postal service should definitely know where the island of Cyprus is, just in case (among other reasons) anyone would ever want to mail anything there. So when An Post, the Irish postal service, issued a commemorative stamp in May 2004 honoring the ten new members of the European Union, some folks couldn't help but notice that Cyprus, one of the new members, was represented on the stamp by an island shaped like Crete, another Mediterranean island that is part of Greece, a current EU member not being honored on the stamp.

An Post spokesperson Anna McHugh quickly moved to suggest that the long, thin, rather Crete-ish island positioned where Crete would be on most maps was actually the rather more squat island of Cyprus: "That really is meant to represent Cyprus, but we've had to take some cartographic license. We simply didn't have room," she said. "Cartographic license" in this case being an "industry term" meaning "We screwed up royally but don't want to admit it." Well, we bet that doesn't make the Cypriots feel better about being represented by a completely different island that is part of an entirely different country. Perhaps Ireland wouldn't mind if Cyprus issued a stamp and represented the Emerald Isle by the island that now hosts England, Scotland, and Wales. Yes, we imagine that'd go over just *fabulously*.

Another interesting bit from the stamp: the Irish island seems to have lost the border between Ireland and Northern Ireland, a cartographic flight of fancy that didn't go over particularly well north of the border. Steven King, an adviser to the Ulster Unionist Party in Belfast, mailed An Post a copy of the 1998 peace treaty that allowed for Northern Ireland to remain part of the United Kingdom, although King allowed the slight probably wasn't intentional: "I'm sure it's just sloppiness. I'm not genuinely offended," he said. "We use British stamps up here anyway."

Sources: Associated Press, BBC

NO STRAIGHT EDGE REQUIRED

Inquiring minds wanted to know: when the Hampshire, England county council authorized county staff to repaint lines in the road East Boldre in the New Forest, why did they make the lines so uneven? It seems that while one of the lines was straight, the other, usually about fifteen feet apart from the first, dipped towards the other lines by a couple of feet in more than one place. The result was very uneven lines on the road. Was this necessary? Did it mean something? Was someone drunk?

"Oh, *those* uneven lines," said the members of the county council. Well, you see, that wavy line is there for safety reasons. Yes, you see, because nothing signals safety like lines making it appear as if the road *narrows*. Well, needless to say, most people weren't quite following the logic for that particular explanation.

So finally the county council cracked and admitted their lie and their mistake. The lines were uneven because someone couldn't read the plans. Council leader Ken Thorber owned up to it to the local press, "What we really wanted was simple straight parallel lines, one down each side of the road 480 cm [that's about 15 feet] apart. Unfortunately there was a problem with the drawings which were badly folded and creases made some of the measurements look like 430 cm [14 feet] and 420 cm [13 feet] instead. The painter followed the instruction which resulted in a straight line down one side of the road and a wavy one down the other."

Good thing the plans weren't crumpled. The lines might have lead directly into *trees*.

Source: Ananova

ARE YOU THERE, VISHWAKARMA? IT'S ME, YADAV

It's probably not easy being the railways minister for the country of India. The rail system in the world's second most populous country has more than 60,000 miles of rail, much of which is old, unreliable, and in nasty state of disrepair. With 300 accidents a year in the system, nearly every day brings news of troubles small and large, and every now and again you get a real whopper, like a train hitting a boulder and derailing in 2004, an accident that killed 20 and injured 100. What a boulder was doing on the tracks is a question for another day.

And perhaps this is why in July 2004, India's railway minister announced that he was no longer responsible for the safety of India's rails. And he named a new executive to take charge of this thorny problem, one who, presumably, would have the resources to handle the needs of India's 13 million daily train-going passengers: Vishwakarma, the Hindu god of machines and draftsman for the entire universe. "Indian Railways are the responsibility of Lord Vishwakarma," said Laloo Prasad Yadav, in passing the rupee. "So is the safety of passengers. It is his duty, not mine."

Well, okay, but how does one let Vishwakarma *know* about the various day-to-day infrastructure needs of the nation's rail lines? Well, see, this is where Minister Yadav apparently springs into action, by talking to a picture of Vishwakarma he has placed on the wall. "I keep telling Him whatever accident or incident takes place on the tracks is His responsibility," Yadav said.

So how did the locals react to Yadav's ideas about personal responsibility? Not very well. Columnist Varghese K. George agreed that the rail system was a national nightmare, but described Yadav's rationalism as "an ingenuous excuse." *Times of India* journalist Manisha Prakash bemoaned the fact that "Gone are the days when railway ministers used to resign, owning responsibility for train mishaps."

So what to do the next time you find yourself on a train in India? Well, obviously, pray. Think of it as speaking directly to the CEO.

Source: *The Times of India, The Indian Express, The Telegraph* (UK)

DOWNGRADING FROM THE SIXTH CIRCLE OF HELL TO THE FIFTH

Something that's always puzzled us is why do people try to scam money from the poor? It's not like they have a whole lot to begin with. And also, it's just plain mean. You're a criminal and you scam a rich person out of $100, and that's just drinks and a cab ride home. Scam a poor person out of $100, and you make them choose between electricity and macaroni and cheese for a month. Really, that's a mark against your soul. We're not afraid to say it.

Also, on a more *practical* level, scamming the poor while working among people who are paid to *help* the poor is not a smart idea and certainly not an ethical one. It tripped up "Marcie," an office clerk who worked at Florida's Department of Children & Families. Marcie's coworkers suspected something was fishy when people who were in need of the department's services would come in and ask to speak to Marcie, whose job description did not include working directly with department clients.

One internal investigation later, the department discovered that Marcie had worked out a neat little scam in which she charged people hundreds of dollars for department services, mostly relating to government-assisted housing, that they were actually eligible for free of charge. Among her victims: a disabled woman, a single mother of three, and a little old lady whose husband had terminal cancer. Marcie scammed an extra C-note out of the little old lady by promising to help get more medical treatment for her husband. All together now: Boooo, Marcie! Boooo!

Marcie was arrested on six counts of unlawful compensation for official behavior and one count of organized fraud and held on $125,000 bail. She's looking at 95 years in the clink. So ironically, it looks like at least one person *will* get government-assisted housing through her efforts.

Source: Associated Press, *Sun-Sentinel* (Fort Lauderdale, FL)

CAN'T BLAME THEM FOR TAKING IT

Georgia's low-income tax credits are designed to give the state's poorest a little bit of a leg up. It's not much—$26 per family member at most—but if you're not making much money, $26 is nothing to sneeze at. Who is eligible for the low-income tax credits? Households with income of less than $20,000 dollars a year. Just like the ones headed up by prisoners.

Yes, prisoners. In 2003 alone, about 200 incarcerated guests of the state of Georgia have found a way to get a little scratch from their jailers, by claiming a low-income tax credit. After all, they *are* making less than $20,000 a year—if you're doing time in a Peach State big house, in fact, chances are you're making nothing at all. And while most people would not consider an 8-by-10-foot cell with an exposed, seatless toilet a household, for the State of Georgia, home is where you lay your hat. Or hide your shiv. Sadly, you can't claim your bunkmate as a dependent.

Georgia legislators are working to close the loophole that allows prisoners to claim the credit, noting that one of the reasons they can claim the credit at all is because they've become wards of the state. Even so, state revenue officials estimate that over the last five years more than $20,000 in credits has gone to incarcerated filers. We wonder how many of them were in for tax fraud.

Source: Atlanta *Constitution-Journal*

BRITAIN, AUSTRIA, LUVANIA?

Quick: Can you name the ten countries that were added to the European Union in May 2004? If you're a citizen of the United States, a likely answer to this question is "The European Whos-whats-nitz, now?" And that's an entirely just answer: Europe is an entire ocean away, after all, and the people there frequently don't even have the courtesy to speak American (the nerve!). You can't reasonably be expected to tell your Slovakias from your Slovenias, and if you can, well, most Europeans would be pleasantly surprised, sort of like they would be by a brown bear that could tie its own shoes.

So if Americans are off the hook, what about the Britons? The UK is *in* the EU, after all, even if it's not so keen on the euro replacing the pound sterling. Surely the average Brit knows the names of the new EU members??

Well, now, not exactly. Just as American's have a hard time telling apart all those countries in Eastern Europe, so apparently do the Brits. Telecommunication provider One.Tel polled 2,500 Brits right around the time the new member states joined the EU and asked them to name the new members from a short list of European countries. Among the Estonias and Latvias and Lithuanias, One.Tel slipped in a ringer: "Luvania," a country that could share a border with Freedonia and possibly Brigadoon.

Despite the absolute fictionality of Luvania, no less than 8 percent of poll respondents identified it as one of the new members of the EU. Moving out of Eastern Europe and heading west, another 15 percent managed to identify Austria as a real country (regrettable past episodes of *Anschluss* notwithstanding) and a member of the EU, which is good, but also believed it was one of the new inductees. This would no doubt come as a surprise to the homeland of Mozart, which had been laboring under the impression it has been an EU member since 1995.

Say what you will about these folks, at least they hazarded a guess, which is more than 40 percent of poll respondents managed to accomplish; they had no idea which countries were being added to the EU and apparently couldn't be bothered to care. Which seems darn uncharitable, from this side of the Atlantic. What if people from California didn't know about Rhode Island? Or Pennsylvania? Or the great state of New Jefferson? It'd be madness! Madness!

Source: One.Tel

The Annals of Ill-Advised Television

TODAY'S EPISODE:
PINK LADY ... AND JEFF

Starring in this Episode: Pink Lady (singers Keiko Masuda and Mitsuyo Nemoto) and Jeff Altman

Debut Episode: March 1, 1980, on NBC

The Pitch: It was the *Sonny and Cher Comedy Hour* for the '80s. The show was the brainchild of NBC head Fred Silverman, who as it happened had been head of programming at CBS when Sonny and Cher did their popular show. Pink Lady was a massive success in their homeland of Japan (the kids loved them!) and Silverman was absolutely sure they would be the next big thing here in the States. One minor problem: neither member of Pink Lady spoke a word of English. Enter comedian Jeff Altman, as their "guide" to all things American.

It Seemed Like a Good Idea at the Time Because: You got us. Two of your three stars can't speak a word of English? What could *possibly* go wrong? On a bright note, each episode ended with everyone in a hot tub.

In Reality: First mistake—cute as the members of Pink Lady were, there's only so far you can go with "Japanese vixens who don't speak a word of English being led around by a comedian" shtick. Second mistake—the show was scheduled opposite *The Dukes of Hazzard,* a show popular with boys in full flower of pubescence, so a key demographic was already otherwise engaged. Third mistake—the variety show format has already been brutally murdered in the late '70s. TV audiences were no longer willing to accept show that feature both Red Buttons and Alice Cooper in the same zip code, much less the same stage.

How Long Did It Last? Five episodes; a sixth was filmed but never aired (it is, however, available on DVD). It's a testament to how forgettable the series was that most people today know of it not from its original run but from a *Saturday Night Live* satire of it called "Pink Lady and Carl," in which pop scientist Carl Sagan is substituted for Jeff. That one SNL sketch was funnier than the entire run of the *Pink Lady* series.

Were Those Responsible Punished? Were they ever. NBC honcho Fred Silverman got the boot (*Pink Lady . . . and Jeff* was just one of many horrifying NBC flops that year), while Jeff Altman's career was sucked into a whirling vortex of obscurity from which it has yet to emerge (he is, however, available for your next special event—really, that's what it says on his Web site). Pink Lady returned to Japan and broke up in 1981; both tried their hand at acting in Japan but reformed in 1997 and in 2003 to release singles and tour Japan.

CHAPTER 7

Hi-TECH HALF-WiTS

People sure have a love-hate relationship with technology: when we score something sweet on eBay, we love it. When the computer swallows half of our book manuscript and we have to make up a barely-plausible lie to our editor about what happened to the half of the book we owe her, well, then, quite obviously, we hate it (please don't tell our editor about the lie about the manuscript. It's just between us).

Just because something is hi-tech and gee-whiz, doesn't mean that it can't be used stupidly—which brings us to this chapter, in which technology is used in ways that would shame those that thought it up.

AND YET, ALMOST
NOTHING OF ANY VALUE
EVER GETS SAID THAT WAY

We've long passed the point where the Guinness World Records have simply become utterly ridiculous; when there is an actual world record for Farthest Spaghetti Nasal Ejection (7.5 inches, held by one Kevin Cole of Carlsbad, New Mexico, whose mother, we're sure, must be prouder than spit), it may be time to pack it in.

Nevertheless, a new and particularly useless world record caught our eye recently: the world record for SMS messaging—that's sending a message using the keypad of a cellular phone for those of you who are still living in the age where all phones did was transmit voices. Today's kids spend a lot of time bumping into things because they're trying to send text messages and walk at the same time.

In June 2004, Singapore (where four out of five people have a cell phone, and that fifth person is talked about disparagingly) hosted 125 competitors who limbered up their fingers to tap out the following 160-character message in the shortest amount of time:

> "The razor-toothed piranhas of the genera Serrasalmus and Pygocentrus are the most ferocious freshwater fish in the world. In reality they seldom attack a human."
> (We knew that.)

When the smoke cleared, the winner was 23-year-old Kimberly Yeo, who hammered out the message in just 43.24

seconds. That was a full 23 seconds faster than the previous record holder, Briton James Trusler. However, Yeo's time was only .2 seconds faster than the runner-up, 18-year-old Ashley Tan, proving that if SMS messaging ever becomes an Olympic sport Singapore will have the Dream Team.

What is this skill actually good for? Aside from passing along information about the dietary habits of certain piranha species, not a whole lot. And of course, the fact that you can say the above factoid into your cell phone several times faster than you can type it seems to have escaped everyone's attention entirely. Nevertheless, previous record holder James Trusler is already gearing up to reclaim his title, stating: "I'm very positive that I can break this record." Live that dream, James! At least it's better than blowing pasta out your nose.

Source: *The Straits Times* (Singapore)

GPS ALSO STANDS FOR "GENERALLY PRETTY STUPID"

Cars these days are so packed with nifty technical gadgets that it's a rare individual who can keep himself from fiddling around with them to try to see how they all work. But some people, especially George Sam Youssef of Australia, might be better off not touching the tech.

One day, Youssef decided to buy a replica pistol in Brisbane, and then use it to carjack a very nice, very expensive BMW. And why stop there? Youssef's next stop was a bank, which he robbed to the tune of $10,000 Australian.

Then he dumped the car and took a bus headed out of town—but not before fiddling with the BMW's Global Positioning system, into which he had entered his father's address, making it a lot easier to track him down. It also didn't help that Youssef's fingerprints were all over the car.

At his trial, the defense tried to gain leniency through the innovative strategy of admitting Youssef's utter lack of criminal skills; "He would have to be one of the most inept armed robbers to come before a court," said defense barrister Mal Harrison, after his client pled guilty to deprivation of liberty, entering a vehicle and unlawful use of a vehicle with aggravation (that'd be the carjacking), as well as robbery with aggravation (for that bank episode).

A bold maneuver! Which didn't work, as Youssef was then sentenced to six years in the pen. They won't need a GPS to find him now.

Source: news.com.au, abc.net.au

THE ULTIMATE
iN POOR SERVICE

We've all heard stories of shifty waiters and waitresses taking down credit card numbers from customers and then using them to buy toys, houses, and ponies. But generally there should be a short interval between the theft of a card number and the accrual of aberrant charges—say, at least a couple of hours. Don't thieves know it's good manners to let your stomach settle before hitting you with the charges?

Someone tell that to "Sheng" and "Han," two waiters from Shanghai. They were waiting on a customer in the restaurant where they worked when Mr. Customer handed over a credit card to pay for lunch. Shortly thereafter, the two of them told Mr. Customer that there was a problem with the receipt, and it would take a couple minutes for them to resolve it. And then shortly after that, Mr. Customer got a call on his cell phone; it was his credit card company, and they wanted to know if he in fact just now purchased $3,000 worth of cell phones. Well, no, he hadn't; he'd just bought lunch. But he could guess who it was *trying* to buy the phones. Sheng and Han were picked up and charged with theft not long after that.

What we want to know is, did Mr. Customer then have to pay for his lunch? And did he leave a tip? We're guessing no on both counts.

Source: CBS News

WIRELESS YET STUPID

As any geek will tell you, the hot trend in home computer geekery is wireless networks: with just a couple of wireless cards and about a day and a half of screaming technological hairpulling before you give up and pay your nephew a case of Mountain Dew to set everything up, you can compute effortlessly anywhere in your house, without wires. Truly, never have so many done so much in order to play online poker in so many nooks and crannies of the house.

But there's a dark side to wireless networking. If you're not careful and don't protect your connection, people can log into it anonymously and use it to do all sorts of bad things. Like Myron Tereshchuk, a fellow from Maryland who had it in for MicroPatent, a company in Connecticut. Tereshchuk believed the firm was in someway responsible for some of the misfortunes his own business had, and took to sending the company threatening e-mails and extortion demands.

Normally something like that would be traceable—to be technical about it, you could look at the e-mail header and see the path the e-mail took from the sending computer to the receiving computer. But Tereshchuk masked his identity by driving around the Washington, DC, area and looking for unsecured wireless networks to log into; when he found one, he'd use it to mail off his threats. These and other tactics kept Tereshchuk one step ahead of the company he was trying to blackmail.

So, yes, Tereshchuk did a fine job in covering his tracks on the technical front. But when it came to other aspects of identity obscuring, he was, well, *less* "ept." For example, there was that time he decided to attempt to extort $17 million from the MicroPatent, or else he'd release some corporate secrets he'd recovered; he demanded the company cut a check payable to "Myron Tereshchuk." As they say, this was the big break investigators were looking for.

One wonders why a man whose desire for anonymity caused him to drive around a major metropolitan area looking for home networks to hack into would suddenly just plop his name out there like fool. We suppose when $17 million is on the line, people's thinking just gets a little fuzzy.

Armed with a big fat honkin' clue like Tereshchuk's name, the FBI began following him around (at one point noting observing him driving erratically as he paid attention to something in the passenger seat—driving and Web browsing don't mix) and eventually got a warrant for his house. Inside they found evidence linking him to the harassment of MicroPatent, as well as some other interesting goodies, like grenades and a recipe for ricin, a nasty poison. Clearly this fellow was just a ball of fun. Tereshchuk was hauled in and eventually pled guilty to "attempted extortion affecting commerce."

Oh well. It was a good plan. A technologically sneaky plan. Too bad the weakest link in Tereshchuk's plan was himself.

Source: *The Register* (UK), U.S. Department of Justice

INSERT "FAVA BEANS AND A NICE CHIANTI" JOKE HERE

Every now and again—by which you can understand to mean probably every fifteen seconds—some idiot somewhere in the world gets the bright idea to put up a joke auction listing on eBay, the world's largest online auction site. Because who doesn't enjoy a good joke auction?

Well, we have two reasons to not file a joke auction on eBay. The first, of course, is that every joke auction eventually has to be taken down by some tech geek at eBay whose very expensive degree in information systems technology is being used to delete an attempt at auction-based humor. So whether or not the joke succeeds in being funny, removing it certainly isn't the high point of the tech's day.

Also, there's the outside chance that some profoundly creepy person won't think your auction is a joke at all. Just ask Daniel O'Dee, a Brit who apparently got a little soused and thought it would be a hoot to auction his body on eBay. Well, quickly enough, the eBay techs took down the auction, but they weren't fast enough on the draw; in O'Dee's e-mail queue was a note from "Donnie, the Hanover Cannibal," who, unaware that the body O'Dee was offering was his very own, offered £2,000 for what Donnie believed was a corpse. Donnie hinted darkly at a cabal of continental cannibals who pooled their resources for fresh human corpses and were interested in O'Dee's dead body auction.

O'Dee, almost certainly creeped out beyond all sensibility, responded to the Hanover homophage that the auction had been for his own body and was just a joke. The Hanover Cannibal's response: "I'm disappointed that is was your own body you were selling as I want one as soon as possible. If you have any other access to a fresh corpse I would be interested. I guarantee that it will be more than a fair price." O'Dee didn't respond to this message, which apparently the Cannibal thought to be rude; Donnie then sent a death threat. Quoth O'Dee to the local paper: "I'm trying to put it out of my mind. It's safe to say I won't be visiting Germany."

Now, of course, it's entirely possible that Donnie the Cannibal is just some dude jerking O'Dee's chain. But, you know, what if he *wasn't*? The correct response to *that,* and we say this with a full measure of masculinity, is "*Eek*!"

So please, no fake eBay auctions. Do it for your soul and those nice eBay techs. Not to mention your liver, your heart and other edible portions of your body.

Source: thisisplymouth.co.uk, United Press International

THE PERILS OF BEING "LEET"

We feel pretty strongly about this: unless you are in fact an elite computer hacker (or, "l337 h4xx0r" as the online community likes to spell it these days), don't go out of your way to *represent* yourself as an elite computer hacker. It's only going to end in pain, and possibly a prison term.

Exhibit #1 is Simon Jones, of Southhampton, England. By day, our friend Mr. Jones was a supermarket shelf-stacker. Ah, but at night! At night he was—well, a supermarket shelf stacker as well. However, he *also* happened to be a supermarket shelf-stacker with a science degree, which is to say, someone who possibly expected something else from his professional career than stacking cans of peas. Not that there's anything *wrong* with stacking peas—someone has to do it, and we're glad they do, since it makes the canned peas easier to find—but you don't actually need a science degree to do it.

And so, not unlike a misunderstood scientist in a comic book whose squashed dreams drive him to a life of crime, Simon Jones found himself planning mischief online. His target: Playboy, an institution founded on the principle of showing nubile young women in various states of undress. Was Simon planning to use his mad hacker "skillz" to tunnel into Playboy's online subscriber database, holding it at ransom until a terrified Hugh Hefner shelled out cash and bunnies? Well, no. Jones's "skillz" were apparently more modest than that. What he *did* have, though, were passwords to Playboy accounts that he found somewhere online, and from his lair (better known as his bedroom in his parent's house), he used those to "prove" to Playboy that he was an elite hacker called "PayMaster 69" who was just itchin' to expose Playboy's subscriber database.

Now, here's why you don't pose as an elite hacker, unless you are, because you'll always give yourself away, like Jonesy here. First, elite hackers don't use their personal email accounts to mail the blackmail notes, like Jones did, since they're pretty easy to trace. Second, if you're not an elite hacker, then you probably don't know what the going rate for online extortion is and may underbid: which is why, we suspect, Jones apparently was tickled when Playboy electronically wired him £60—about $100—as his "payment."

Third, if you're not an elite hacker, you may not know how to hide what money you've extorted. Jones certainly didn't; he transferred the money into his personal bank account, which, electronically speaking, is like sending up a flare so the appropriate authorities can bear down on you like a cadre of hawks on a field mouse.

So, no real surprise that shortly after Jones's extravagant £60 extortion payday, his parents' home was the recipient of a pre-dawn raid by members of both U.S. Secret Service agents *and* officers from the UK's National Hi-Tech Crime Unit. From there it was just a hop, skip, and a jump to two years in prison. Jones's lawyer suggested Jones had been bored and committed the crime just for fun and not financial gain. This is an interesting argument—that attempting to extort a large corporation is fine as long as you're just doing it for kicks and giggles. In this case, the judge wasn't buying it. "You were bored and disappointed you had not found employment in the computer world as you hoped," the judge told Jones. "But this was a planned invasion. Your e-mail to Playboy set out your motive to extract money." And off to the slammer he went.

Interestingly, Jones's science degree will be even less useful to him behind bars than it was stocking shelves. In the words of the hackers, he's been "0wnz0red" (which for us lay-people simply means "screwed").

Source: *The Telegraph* (UK), *The Register* (UK)

BiDDiNG ON JAiL TiME

On one hand, eBay is a great way to get a whole bunch of crap you don't actually *need* without pathetically cruising your hometown looking for yard sales. On the other hand, it's a fine way to drive yourself utterly insane when you get trapped in a bidding war with some fool who doesn't realize that that collection of *Speed Racer* posable figures was meant to be owned by you and you *alone.* The next thing you know you've spent a third of your monthly take-home on tchotckes that would fetch no more than 25 cents at a swap meet. Isn't technology *wonderful?*

eBay rage will sometimes drive losing bidders to more frightening extremes. Take the case of "Paul," a New Orleans native who bid on a collection of band uniforms and dance costumes that he figured he could resell at a profit (probably on eBay—because after all, if more than one person bids on something, doesn't it prove there's a market for it?). But, drat it all, there was one obstacle between Paul and his dream of slightly used epaulet-bearing clothing: "Chuck," in New York, who was bidding on the same lot of uniforms. And when all was said and done and the dust had cleared on the virtual bidding floor, it was Chuck who came away with all 480 pieces of band/dance paraphernalia, at the price of $360.

Well, Paul must of heard of that famous salesman maxim: "Everything is open to negotiation," because rather than accept his defeat and find something else to bid on, Paul began to badger Chuck directly through e-mail and by phone to sell the aforementioned auction winnings to him. Alas, Chuck liked his band clothes so much that he would not part with a single stitch, at least not to Paul. So Paul decided it was time for more, shall we say, *dramatic* methods of persuasion. He took a train from New Orleans to New York, then allegedly broke into Chuck's house, and threatened Chuck's wife with a gun; Chuck was not home at the time.

Well, Mrs. Chuck held on to her husband's winnings, and Paul left without the precious band uniforms. Chuck's wife then called the police, who picked up Paul in a taxi he was taking back to the train station. When the police questioned Paul about the incident, apparently he didn't deny showing up at Chuck's house, but he did dispute the "waving the gun around" part. The gun just happened to fall out of his briefcase, he said. This leaves open the question of why there was a gun in his briefcase at all, but let's leave that now. A better question is why was Paul willing to pay $300 to go from New Orleans to New York by train (as was the going price when we checked while writing this) just to wheedle Chuck out of his band uniforms? Why he didn't just kick in an extra $5 to top Chuck's bid in the first place?

That extra $5 could have saved Paul a lot more than the cost of a train ticket: Paul was charged with burglary, coercion, and criminal possession of a weapon, which mean if he's found guilty he's going to spend at least five years in the state pen. Which seems a pretty steep price for band uniforms, even by eBay standards.

Source: Court TV

NO SUCH THING
AS A FREE FILL-UP

We don't want to suggest gas prices were high in 2004, but when people started offering up their first-borns for a full tank, it began to get a little bit crazy. That being the case, one is not entirely unsympathetic to the 107 people who used an interesting glitch in a magic Michigan gas pump to drive away with free gasoline.

At this particular pump, in Pittsfield Township, someone made the discovery that if you fed it a Michigan driver's license instead of a credit card, it would let you take as much gas as you liked. Michigan licenses, like credit cards, have magnetic data strips on the back, which is apparently what confused the poor automated gas pump. But since the license isn't set up to be charged for purchases, the gas you pumped ended up being free. And who doesn't like free?

Well, the owners of the gas pump for one, and the local law enforcement for another. Both of these considered the folks who took free gas to be—what's the word in English? Oh yes, that's right—thieves. And here's the kind of amusing thing about the whole "use your drivers license instead of your credit card" scam: while a Michigan driver's license isn't set up to be charged for gas, it *is* set up to transmit the information on your driver's license, like your name and address. Which is what it did, handing that information right to the police. You would think that some of those people swiping a government-issued ID to steal gas would have thought about that tiny detail. Apparently not.

All of those people who came in for free gas—some of whom filled up as much as fifteen times in three weeks—are going to end up paying one way or another. Let's hope the cops let them resolve it with a credit card. A real one, this time.

Source: *Boston Globe*

CELL PHONE CRAZINESS

Who among us who has a cell phone has not had the urge to throw the thing as far as its tiny little clamshell body could be hurled? If it's not spotty coverage, it's random roaming charges or the fact in so many places you can get *ticketed* by the police for nothing more than your right to blab away on the phone while driving your two-ton SUV at 80 miles an hour down the highway. As if anything *bad* might happen.

Well, here's what we say: if you're that angry with your phone, chuck that baby as far as you can. Catharsis is good, if somewhat expensive. However—and this is key—throw only *your* phone. Start throwing somebody else's phones, and then you might have a problem.

"Hal" of Fargo, North Dakota, recently learned this lesson when he stomped into a Verizon Wireless store with the intent of registering a complaint about his cell phone service. Well, actually, he wasn't planning on just dropping off a sternly worded letter of complaint. As he admitted to a local paper, his plan was to go in there and actually yell at people. But he just couldn't stick to the plan. "I just lost it," he later admitted. "I just started grabbing computers and phones and throwing them. I just destroyed the place . . . I kind of regret that I did it, but I hope my message got across." Oh, we bet they could hear him now.

Possibly, but more likely the message the employees of the store were receiving was: there's a crazed idiot in the store, which is why, not long after one of the employees was beaned in the shoulder with a hurled communications device, they holed themselves up in a back office and called the police. Hal, his rage apparently spent, was arrested without incident and charged with felony criminal mischief and misdemeanor simple assault. It is our suspicion he won't have to worry about roaming charges for some time.

Source: CNN

SLEEP ON YOUR OWN TIME, BUB

Want to make people in a rail yard nervous? It's simple. Just put something in the rail yard that's not supposed to be there. After the terrible bombing of a train in Madrid, Spain, in March 2004, anything unusual in a train yard is automatically suspicious, and of course, anything suspicious is automatically bad.

This is why the police in Philadelphia, Pennsylvania, and the FBI were very, very nervous about the object they found at a commuter rail yard in Philadelphia in May 2004. It was a motion detector—a small monitor that lets someone know about comings and goings in the yard. It was found by a conductor and turned over to a police officer (who, in an entirely different dumb act that we'll leave largely unconsidered, kept the thing in his locker for a week before turning it over to his bosses). No one knew where it had come from; no one knew what it meant. The local media had a field day speculating about its possible terrorist origins, which undoubtedly made the thousands who daily rode the rails oh *so* secure.

But finally the truth was revealed. The motion sensor was not placed in the rail yard by terrorists but by an employee of the rail yard, specifically an electrician. Why did he put in the rail yard? Because he wanted a nap. With the sensor in place, the electrician would be alerted when his boss was on the way over—he could wake up totally refreshed and look like he'd been busy at work all that time. It would have been positively ingenious, had not all of Western Civilization been spooked about possible acts of terrorism.

The electrician was not immediately fired, but as the chief of security for the Southeastern Pennsylvania Transportation Authority rather dryly noted to CBS News, "I think he is about to begin taking vacation time immediately." He should probably catch up on his sleep. He should probably also avoid traveling by train.

Source: *The Philadelphia Inquirer,* CBS News

Dim Bulbs in Bright Lights
BEING THERE (1979)

Our Dumb Guy: Chance the Gardener, also known as Chauncey Gardiner (Peter Sellars)

Our Story: A mentally challenged gardener (Sellars) lives his whole life in the Washington, DC, townhouse of his boss. After the boss's death, Chance must go out in to the world. There he meets a politically connected billionaire (Melvyn Douglas) and his wife (Shirley MacLaine), who befriend him and take his naive, TV-derived utterances as profound wisdom. Soon, Chance is the toast of the District and may eventually become a political power of his own, even if he has no idea what that means.

Dumb or Stoned? Definitely not stoned, just a simple man, with a simple life philosophy.

High Point of Low Comedy: Shirley MacLaine's character attempts to seduce Chance, who is far more interested in watching the television, which leads to some very amusing calisthenics.

And Now, In His Own Words: Chance, upon riding in a car for the first time: "This is just like television, only you can see much further."

He's Dumb, But Is the Film Good? It's better than good. It's one of the best films of its year, and features one of Peter Sellars's best performances, dumb or otherwise. This is high praise when you consider he plays one of the greatest "dumb" film characters of all time, Inspector Clouseau. It's also a fine example of how you can have a very smart movie about very smart things and still have a complete idiot as the main character.

CHAPTER 8

A HUNK, A HUNK OF BURNIN' DUMB

Greek mythology tells the tale of Prometheus, who saw poor little humans shivering in the dark and stole fire from the gods to give to man. And for this he was severely punished by the gods. We imagine Prometheus reading this next chapter and saying, "For this, I was chained to a rock?" Yes you were, Prometheus. And we're sorry.

Of course, fire is like any tool; it's all in how you use it. Fire can keep you warm, or it can burn down your house. But fire wants to be useful, not destructive. Consider it an unwitting accomplice in what follows.

TALK ABOUT CHAR-BROILED

Jerry" had a beef with Burger King; he wasn't getting enough hours as an employee. He just didn't feel valued. And who hasn't been in those shoes?

Now, when you feel you aren't being valued as an employee, and are not getting enough hours thereby, there are several things you can do to remedy the situation: offer to work late hours, perhaps, or early ones. Let your coworkers know you'd be willing to stand in for them if they need extra time off. Or convince your manager, through the cunning use of pie charts, that you were indeed ready, willing, and able to take up those extra hours.

But Jerry chose a different route; allegedly, he went into his place of work in Dorset, England, chose a nice bin full of hamburger wrappers, and set them ablaze. And then started eight more fires in and around the store. And then he stood back and watched his coworkers run around, futilely trying to extinguish the flames before the building had to be evacuated. In addition to causing more than $1 million in damage and gutting the restaurant, the fire put forty people out of work, including Jerry. And now he's getting no hours! So you see the true flaw in the plan. Well, that and the not-insignificant detail that Jerry was then charged with arson, which really doesn't look good on a resume.

Of course, where Jerry is likely going, he's going to get plenty of hours. The pay's not so good. And it's doubtful after this, they'll let him work in the kitchen.

Source: *The Sun* (UK)

CRISPY CRITTERS,
CRISPY COMMERCE

We understand that people don't like spiders. Helpful and useful though they are (imagine how many flies there'd be without them hanging around), they are *creeeeeeeeepy*, what with those eight twitchy legs and eight twitchy eyes and that freaky, skittering thing they do across walls. Really, *ick*. Lots of people are none too keen to have eight-legged creepy crawlies around their workspace and will do just about anything to be spider-free.

May we suggest, however, in your rush to exterminate the area's spider population, that you avoid setting them aflame. The reason we suggest this is that we're reading the story of "Pauly," an assistant manager at the Champs Sports store in the Oakdale Mall of Johnson City, New York. Seems that Pauly, no fan of the arachnids, took extreme umbrage at a representative of that order hanging around in his store. Rather than stomp it with the no-doubt numerous cross-training shoes he had on hand, he decided to torch the creepy-crawly instead. And so Pauly sprayed it with a flammable substance, set it on fire, and then, we're sure, leaned in to hear the little tiny screams.

There was screaming, all right. You see, the fire was not content merely to burn alive a small arthropod; no, it wanted more, like the merchandise in the storage area, and then the store itself. Other people in the mall couldn't help but notice the flames and smoke and heat, so in short order people fled from their shopping as fast as their legs would carry them.

Smoke was visible from more than a mile away. Aside from the Champs, which naturally experienced severe fire damage, followed by significant water damage (when the firefighters arrived), several other shops suffered slight to moderate damage. Pauly was charged with fourth-degree arson, which is a felony.

So in one flaming maneuver, he killed both a spider *and* his retail career. That takes real talent. Somewhere in spider heaven, an eight-legged angel is snacking on a fly and having a good, long laugh.

Source: *Press & Sun-Bulletin* (Binghamton, NY), *Journal* (Ithaca, NY)

FROM THE DO-AS-WE-SAY-
NOT-AS-WE-DO DEPARTMENT

This is one of those "We're gonna get ribbed about this one for years" stories. In Lancaster, Texas, the firefighters at Station No. 3 got a call to a major accident on Interstate 35. When a call like that comes in, they drop whatever they're doing and get to it, no matter what they are doing at the time.

As people who count on local firefighters to keep our homes from turning into blackened husks, we respect and applaud that sort of thinking; the sooner they get to the scene, the more of our houses will remain after the fire's out. And yet we wonder if there's such a thing as too hasty where firefighting is concerned.

In the case of Station No. 3, they were in such a rush to leave that someone—we're not saying who—left some potatoes cooking on the stove. With no one there to tend the stove, the potatoes started to burn and, before they knew it, there was a fire at the firehouse. Firefighters from other stations responded to the flames (called in by rightfully concerned Lancaster residents), and ended up causing about $125,000 worth of damage.

"I'll bet if you ask, most departments have had this happen," Lancaster Fire Marshall Ladis Barr said. We're pretty sure most fire departments would beg to differ. But at least now you know why you should always pay attention to what you've got cooking on the stove whether you're a firefighter or not!

Source: Dallas *Morning News*

PANTS ON FIRE

We're big believers in practical observation of scientific phenomena; nothing helps you understand things like seeing them happen in the real world. And yet, there are some things we honestly feel we don't need to actually observe to know what the outcome will be. Our predictive abilities, honed by years of training and experience, usually are enough in most cases.

To give an example, let's say you had a container filled with *highly flammable* material. Now, let's suppose you have a pair of pants, and you get some of this *highly flammable* material on those pants—which, we should note, are reasonably *flammable* in and of themselves. Now you've got a *flammable* substance on a *flammable* article of clothing. Okay? Now, what do you think happens to that when you get it near an open flame? If you answered, "Why, I expect it would burn," congratulate yourself, because your predicative ability is of the highest rank—and you didn't have to catch on fire to get your answer.

Alas, "Ricky," a college student working in a California furniture factory, did not have such advanced reasoning skills. And so, when his pants were saturated with a highly flammable chemical used in the manufacture of furniture, he decided he needed to find out what would happen to them if they were exposed to an inflamed cigarette lighter. So, out came the lighter—flick, flick, flick—and then Ricky put the flame to his pants *while still wearing them.*

So what happened? Well, the pants caught on fire, of course, and Ricky, with his pants on fire, suffered minor burns. Also, part of the furniture factory caught fire, which required 30 minutes for firefighters to extinguish. The factory itself sustained minimal damage, but there was some heavily toasted furniture for the employees to haul out over the next few days.

"It just baffles me," said factory business manager Dan Slayton, of Ricky's decision to set his pants and himself on fire. Join the club, Dan. Normally we applaud curiosity, but this time, we figure it was more trouble than it was worth. At least now Ricky knows. And knowing is half the battle, we guess.

Source: *The Union* (Nevada County, CA), United Press International

HE'LL BE THE BUTT
OF JOKES FOR YEARS

There's no possible way we could as succinctly sum up
Jim McGill's incident as well as he did, so let us let him
describe it in his own words: "The bottle rocket exploded on
the launching pad. And the launching pad was my rear end."

Here's the set-up. McGill is a member of a radio station
morning show in Springfield, Illinois, where he is known as
"Jim the Photographer." Part of McGill's gig as a morning
show hanger-on is to do physically humiliating things for the
amusement of the radio audience. In May 2004, he decided to
climb up on top of a radio station's Hummer (that's the vehicle, folks), pull his pants down, and lodge a small tube between his butt cheeks. Then some radio station lackeys had
the dubious honor of stuffing bottle rockets into the tube and
lighting them.

McGill later claimed to have done this stunt dozens of
times before—a fact that must be contemplated for its own
sober horror—without a hitch. But, see, if you spend a lot of
your time launching bottle rockets from your rear, eventually
you're going to get burned. And indeed McGill did: one of
those bottle rockets had a little extra spark to it, and some of
that spark went right down that tube, bathing McGill's tender
bottom in flaming terror. The whole incident, it probably goes
without saying, was broadcast live over the radio. McGill was
rushed to the local hospital and was required to undergo sur-
gery for burns on his buttocks and anus, an excruciatingly
painful fate just to *ponder.*

But wait, here's the *irony:* as McGill has been the (heh) butt of jokes for his radio show before (including a March faked death due to "rectal trauma"), many station listeners apparently refused to believe that McGill was actually injured and that the whole thing was not some elaborate hoax. So kids, don't try this at home. And as for McGill, let's hope he's learned his lesson.

Source: *State Journal-Register* (Springfield, IL)

KEEP THE HOME FIRES BURNING

When wasps decide to take up residence in one's house, a common solution to the problem is to call the friendly neighborhood professional exterminator (not the guy on the street corner who's done time in the big house—we're talking bugs, people), who will often use a sort of smoke to choke the bugs and solve the problem. As with so many things involving fire and dangerous venom-bearing insects, it's probably best to leave these things to the professionals; otherwise it's possible what you'll have on your hands is a pile of smoking rubble that used to be your house.

"Susan," from Penydarrren area of Wales in the United Kingdom, apparently thought that professional bug-killing help was for quitters; any fool could make smoke, and anyway, exterminators cost money. So when wasps set up shop in her house, Sue attempted her own defense of her property. She grabbed some cardboard and then set it aflame. Then, as smoke was what she was after, she blew out the fire and, according to local fire enforcement, set the smoldering cardboard under a board next to the house to smoke out the wasps in her walls.

The flaw in the plan—and you knew there was one—was that the board acted a bit like a chimney and suddenly the smoking cardboard was on fire again. Whoops. The fire sparked the roof timbers and then spread flames that started burning *inside* the walls of her home. Whoops again. Although that's certainly an *interesting* fire, the flames on the roof were easily in evidence but the fire inside the walls, well, call it a stealth fire—one you can't see but which cheerfully destroys your home anyway. It's also a difficult fire for firefighting professionals to get at. The ones that arrived at Sue's home ended up tearing through Susan's walls and ceiling to get to the burning parts. In all it took more than two hours to contain the blaze, and Susan's house had that not-so-great wood-smoked flavor to it when everything was said and done.

The wasps? They were fine, of course. They had to call a professional to get rid of them. Funny how *they* always show up, sooner or later.

Source: BBC

SOME LIFE LEFT IN THEM

Here's something we've learned from researching this particular story: just because that cannonball or artillery shell is really old, doesn't mean it isn't still live ammunition. So be careful with that thing.

The cannonball aspect of our tale comes in from Cape Fear, North Carolina, which has a Civil War museum. It appears that a local contractor had a Civil War-era cannon ball in his possession and thought it would be nice to donate it to the museum. It was indeed a thoughtful gift, but the cannonball came with something extra, namely, a round of shot with an intact fuse, which technically kinda made it a *bomb,* which led to the evacuation of several dozen people and the summoning of the local bomb squad. Whoops.

As bad as that was, the next story tops it: a seventh-grader in Frederick County, Virginia, thought that his civics teacher might be interested in a little bit of family history. So one day, he brought it in to share: a foot-long artillery shell that experts later guessed was of World War I vintage. Before the student could share it with his teacher (and, incidentally, this seems *totally* innocent on the kid's part—it's not like he was planning to blow up the teacher), it was noticed by other staff members. Thus resulted another evacuation scene (this time 1,000 people had to vamoose) and another call to experts in exploding things.

Good news: No one injured in either case. Sometimes you get lucky.

Source: WECT.com, *The Winchester Star*

The Really Stupid Quiz

A HUNK, A HUNK
OF BURNING DUMB

One of these stories is true. Two are not. Pick the right one and you'll be aglow with victory. Choose the wrong one and you'll be burned by defeat.

1. When you get pizza and your dog wants a slice, you know what you should do? Give it to him. If you don't, your dog might "accidentally" burn down the house trying to get some. Which is just what happened in Racine, Minnesota, when a man set a pizza box on the stove, and his pup, in an attempt to get at the pie, accidentally turned on a gas burner. The next thing they knew, the pizza box was on fire, and then so were other parts of the kitchen, and then, we suspect, there was a dog with pizza sauce on its muzzle and its tail tucked in between its legs. Second hint: if you *don't* give your dog pizza, don't put the box on the stove. Or maybe get a Chihuahua. Just a thought.

2. "Timmy," a second-grade student at Melinda Heights Elementary School in Rancho Santa Margarita, California, dreaded showing his report card to his parents; Timmy had gotten several low marks and a disciplinary comment from his teacher. But Timmy reasoned that his parents would never know about those bad grades if the report card didn't exist; so Timmy used his mother's lighter to set his report card on fire. Sadly, Timmy's fire safety education appears to

have been lacking, since he ignited both the report card and the living room drapes. Flames quickly spread to the walls and ceiling. At the end of the day, Timmy's antics caused extensive fire damage throughout the house. Principal Don Snyder noted to reporters that Timmy's effort would have been futile in any event, as student grades are available for parental perusal online.

3. "Jim," of Phoenix, Arizona, thought he had come up with a clever way to propose to his girlfriend in July 2004; he would spray lighter fluid on her lawn to spell out the words "Marry Me Kristi" and then set his question on fire. Maybe it was a bright idea, save for two factors: first, Phoenix is hot and dry in July, which would make the lawn also very dry, kind of like kindling, you might say. Second, Jim had to try twice to write his "marry me" message; according to firefighting personnel on the scene, Jim's first try was misspelled, prompting him to "cross it out" by spewing lighter fluid over the words. As a result, quite a lot of the lawn was primed to go up in flames, which is just what it did. Firefighters called to the scene quickly put out the hot fire of love, but police arrested Jim for destruction of private property. No word on whether Kristi said yes.

Turn to page 329 for the answer.

The Annals of Ill-Advised Television

TODAY'S EPISODE: YOU'RE IN THE PICTURE

Starring in this Episode: The Great One, Jackie Gleason

Debut Episode: January 20, 1961 (coincidentally, the inaugural date of John F. Kennedy) on CBS

The Pitch: It's a gameshow, hosted by Jackie Gleason, one of the great figures in early television (*The Jackie Gleason Show, The Honeymooners*). The premise is a take on an old carnival gag—celebrity guests stick their heads through plywood cutouts in a picture and would then guess what picture they were in as Gleason guided them with hints.

It Seemed Like a Good Idea at the Time Because: Gleason was one of America's most beloved entertainers; Groucho Marx had a not-too-dissimilar personality-driven game show, *You Bet Your Life,* which had been wildly successful.

In Reality: The "celebrities stick their heads through holes" idea probably would have been more amusing if someone were waiting on the other side with a mallet; clips show the first episode as an incoherent mess of cross-talk, over which Gleason would occasionally bellow "Hold it! Wait a minute!" to try to take control of the action. The situation was so awful that the second episode of the show was nothing but Gleason standing up in front of a studio audience and apologizing for the badness of the previous week's show.

How Long Did It Last? Eight weeks. After the apology episode (which was as widely praised as the first episode was panned), Gleason never went back to the game show format. Instead he turned it into a talk show. CBS, not amused, pulled the plug.

Were Those Responsible Punished? Not really. Gleason, who helped create the show, was back on CBS in 1962 with a very successful variety show that ran for nine years. They don't call him The Great One for nothing, you know.

CHAPTER 9

THE LAW IS BLIND, NOT DUMB

We can't exactly say that we're surprised that we found so many examples of dumb people running afoul of the law. Isn't that what the law is for? To catch the dumb and felonious at their own game? (The smart and felonious take a little more work. See your local paper's business section for more details.) So it is with a certain amount of gratification that we provide you with this chapter, which shows you that sometimes the system works!

UNDERCOVER IDIOCY

Ted" was a man undercover. His beat was his neighborhood in Kinston, North Carolina. His quarry—Sam, his neighbor. Oh, Sam was a bad one, all right, and Ted was ready to haul him to the county jail for his crimes. Ted waited until the moment was right and Sam wouldn't be expecting the arrival of *justice*.

Ted waited for the weekend to make his move. Sam was in his yard, washing his tires, when Ted sprang into action and confronted Sam with a big wooden stick and a semiautomatic handgun. Ted informed Sam that he was an undercover agent and that Sam was going down. Even confronted with a stick *and* a gun, though, Sam resisted arrest. But when justice comes calling, you can't reverse the charges! Ted rushed Sam and cuffed him. In no time, Ted got Sam in the back of his car and drove him to the county jail, where he told the authorities that he was charging Sam with various crimes including possession of stolen property and illegal sales of alcohol and lottery tickets.

To which the authorities replied: Hey, *you're* not a cop. *You* can't arrest anyone. But we can arrest *you*. Which is exactly what they did with Ted, charging him with kidnapping, aggravated assault, and possession of a concealed weapon (the gun, we imagine, rather than the stick).

"It was the darnedest thing," said Joe Grady of the Lenoir County Magistrate's office, who was the one who realized Ted was not, in fact, a licensed dispenser of justice. "I've never seen anything like that before."

Source: Associated Press

SOMEONE WHO WOULDN'T BENEFIT FROM TIPS FOR STUPID CRIMINALS

You have to be a pretty bad bank robber when even the judge sentencing you looks upon you as an object of pity. And that's just how bad a robber "Marvin" from Düsseldorf, Germany, was. Don't believe it? Let us regale you with the tale of his utterly incompetent attempt to boost a bank.

His first error was an early arrival to the bank he was planning to rob. He got there *before* it opened and hung around outside. This is a fine way to look awfully suspicious (and in fact, not arriving early to a bank robbery is an actual Tip for Stupid Criminals, which you'll find on page 294). But Marvin didn't go in when they opened the bank. Rather he paced back and forth, Hamlet-like, in front of the bank for three hours, thereby compounding suspicions with his odd behavior.

Finally, Marvin committed himself to a course of action. Bank robbery, here we come! He went into the bank; to mask his identity, he pulled his hat down over his face. Sadly for Marvin, he'd cut eyeholes in the wrong place; now he couldn't see. Apparently frustrated, he ripped the hat off his head—and in the process, gave the bank's security cameras a fine and loving look at his felonious face: the judge at his sentencing would later comment that they were truly "first-class pictures."

After all this Marvin went to a cashier and threatened her so she would cough up the cash. The threat would have been more persuasive if there had been a gun in his hand; instead, Marvin had a gun-shaped cigarette lighter. The cashier, who we suspect at this point felt more pity than fear, suggested to Marvin he might want to, you know, leave. Marvin, utterly defeated, tried to do just that, but as he stepped outside, there were the police, to take him into their tender care.

At his hearing, Judge Wolfram Schnorr gave poor Marvin a one-year suspended sentence and the following piece of advice: "You'd be better off giving up robbing banks. You are clearly untalented for the job." Let's hope for his own sake Marvin takes the judge's advice.

Source: Ananova

YOU'RE NOT AN EMERGENCY!

When you hear stories about 911 calls that have gone **wrong,** it's usually because the person calling for assistance isn't quite clear on the concept of 911. They're calling because they've locked themselves out of their car, or they're wanting the cops to arrest their neighbors for playing their music too loud, or maybe because they're just, you know, *lonely.* But for variety's sake, let's tell you a story where the traditional roles are reversed: real emergency with an idiot 911 operator.

Our story unfolds in Fort Worth, Texas, where members of the Diaz family were somewhat alarmed when intruders attempted to break down their door to gain entry into their home. If ever there's a time to call 911, this is probably it. So one of the Diaz family dialed to get police assistance.

Unfortunately, the 911 operator didn't seem particularly inclined to get the police headed in the Diazs' direction. Instead, she asked them, "OK, who were they? Because strangers don't just come bang down your door with knives," and, "Do you have a brother or father there who they were looking for?" Usually, the operator doesn't try to discern a perpetrator's motives when someone calls for help; one would hope that he or she would just send the police and let the people in the blue uniforms sort it out. But, for some dumb reason, Ms. 911 Operator didn't this time. Instead, she kept them on the line until the Diazs' unidentified door smackers appeared to disperse, refused to pass along information to the police, and suggested to the Diazs that if the bad folks showed up again, they should call back *then.*

Well, another member of the Diaz family did call 911 back about 20 minutes later and luckily found an intelligent operator this time who passed the information on to the police. *That* finally prompted a police visit, followed by a police investigation, of which the preliminary results revealed— surprise!—that the 911 operator who answered the phone the first time wasn't doing her job.

We imagine the next phone call the Diazs will be making is to the lawyers.

Source: WFAA.com

A ONE WAY TICKET TO STUPIDVILLE, FIRST CLASS

Here was "Jeff's" problem. Though he was in Massachusetts, he wanted to go to Cape Verde, the tiny island country off the coast of Senegal, Africa, where he had relatives. There was also the matter of the warrants for his arrest, which we suspect heightened his urge to get away from it all. Alas, being homeless, it was economically beyond his means—it's not as if there are any cheap, direct flights to Cape Verde from Logan International Airport. So Jeff hit upon a plan: why pay for the cost of a plane ticket when he could just *mail* himself to Cape Verde?

Sure, stuffing one's self into a cargo crate might be uncomfortable. But Jeff could prepare himself with a stock of water and food—and a little container or two for the end products of those provisions. He'd be cramped, but he'd end up in Cape Verde. In all, a fine plan. Jeff stuffed himself in a four-by-four foot crate with his supplies (a bag of potato chips, a loaf of bread, a bottle of water, and a bottle for waste) and had some friends seal him up and drop him off at a shipping company in Fall River.

And now—you *knew* it was coming—the flaw in the plan. Clearly, given Jeff's rather small supply of food and drink, he was expecting his crate to be whisked away in a day, maybe two, tops. But the intricacies of maritime shipping were working against our pal Jeff. In fact, there was a two-week wait for the boat to Cape Verde. And then it would be another two weeks for the boat to arrive in Cape Verde. So Jeff would get to Cape Verde, he'd just be dead when he arrived. And wouldn't that be a delightful surprise for the relatives?

Fortunately for Jeff, a few days into his crating, one of his friends came to his or her senses, realized that stuffing a human being into a shipping crate was utterly insane, and called the police, who dispatched officers and dogs to the scene. The shipping company manager was incredulous ("I thought it was a joke," he told the *Providence Journal.* "Someone got inside a box and tried to ship himself? Come on"). Sure enough, the dogs sniffed out the exhausted, dehydrated and only semi-coherent Jeff, who was then uncrated, arrested, and sent to the hospital.

Next time? Fed Ex for sure.

Source: *Boston Globe, Providence Journal*

ATTENTION, WAL-MART SHOPPERS

Shad" **walked into the Naples,** Florida, Wal-Mart one day in search of new clothes and some garbage bags. It wasn't what Shad bought that caught the Wal-Mart workers' attention; after all, Wal-Mart has a wide selection of each item. No, it was the small fact that while Shad was shopping for these items, he just happened to be covered in blood.

Let's do the math here: Blood-soaked Wal-Mart customer + shopping for new clothes + shopping for garbage bags = Deeply suspicious Wal-Mart employees. And rightly so. The fact Shad paid for his purchases with a bloody $100 bill probably didn't do much to ease what suspicions these good folks had.

So after Shad had purchased his things and drove off in a pickup, the employees called the police, who picked up Shad later in the day (after he tried evading arrest, of course). The blood? It probably had something to do with body of a sometime friend of Shad's that the police found. Shad was charged with second-degree murder.

The moral of the story: when you're covered in blood, it's probably not the best time to go shopping.

Source: Associated Press

SHE SHOULD HAVE
SEEN IT COMING

Call us cynical, but all our faith in psychics went out the window when Miss Cleo got busted for fraud. Merely the bust itself was elegant proof of the lack of psychic ability; after all, if she was psychic, how could she *not* know the Feds were on her tail?

But it does seem like some people haven't learned to doubt the powers of psychics, which can be a good thing, especially when those people are drug dealers. One Brooklyn, New York, gang hired "Rosa," to tell them whether certain drug deals were going to go down well. But it seems Rosa wasn't so psychic that she could tell her bosses that their little crew was, in fact, being scoped out by the cops, who in June 2004 slapped down a massive, 133-count indictment against fifteen people, including members of the alleged drug crew. Now, honestly, if a psychic can't see *that* coming, what good is she?

Rosa was so bad at her job that, like Miss Cleo, she didn't even see her own downfall; the cops dropped by her place with a search warrant and then found a box with four handguns. Rosa's comment when the cops found the box: "I always sensed evil in that box." Call us crazy here, but when you sense evil in a box, shouldn't you *drag that box out of your home?* We're just saying. Perhaps Rosa's next trick will be to predict just how much time she'll have in the big house.

Source: CBS News

SERIOUSLY OUT OF UNIFORM

It was bad enough for "Pierre" that he was stopped by the Paris police for driving under the influence. Pierre was a Parisian policeman himself. What made it worse was that when Pierre was stopped, he was out of uniform. *Waaaay* out of uniform. As in, the only thing Pierre was wearing was a pair of fishnet tights.

Although there were undoubtedly a number of plausible lies Pierre could have uttered to explain his attire ("My car's air-conditioning was out," or even "What sort of world do we live in where an off-duty Parisian cop *can't* drive around wearing only fishnet tights?"), Pierre instead went for the career-torpedoing truth. Not only was he a cop, he was also a part-time prostitute. This explanation made sense considering Pierre was apprehended after a chase through the *Bois de Boulogne,* a wooded area on the Paris outskirts long rumored to be the place to go when you're looking for transsexual hookers.

Oddly enough, even though Pierre admitted to a little illegal moonlighting hooking for extra scratch, the police court prosecutors claimed there was not enough evidence to try him for "passive soliciting," which as far as we can tell means he could keep his badge. But that matter of driving drunk could cost Pierre his driver's license. Then he'd have to use public transportation to get to his second job. Wonder if he'd be willing to wear only fishnets on the bus.

Source: Reuters

THAT'S THE TICKET

Normally we're all for our policemen and women being enthusiastic about their work, but we'd like to remind the esteemed members of the law enforcement community who happen to be reading this book that although law enforcement is many things, one thing it is not is a competitive sport. Start trying to one-up each other, and it's going to end badly for someone, usually someone who is presumed to be innocent until proven otherwise.

Come with us now to the Georgia town of Porterdale, where on February 16, 2004, the traffic court, normally a fairly staid and quiet place, was suddenly swamped with crushes of ticketed citizens there for their allotment of justice. Confused by the swarm of malefactors, officials checked the tickets and discovered two interesting things: First, the number of tickets issued in January was up 140 percent from the usual monthly average, and second, the majority of the tickets—150 out of 240—were written up by two of the town's officers, who we will dub Officers "Chip" and "Dale."

Were officers Chip and Dale just incredibly attentive and efficient in their jobs? Perhaps. But perhaps there was also something to the fact that earlier, Judge C. David Strickland recalled hearing a conversation between the two in which they were bragging about how many tickets they'd given out. Seems there was something of a wager on the side as to who could churn out the most tickets. As it happened, both Chip and Dale tied with 75 tickets, many of which were tied to offenses Porterdale mayor Paul Oeland described as "petty in nature." We suspect they were probably petty in intent as well.

What did officers Chip and Dale win for their efforts? Well, first they got to see most of their citations thrown out by the same judge who overheard the two of them bragging about their ticketing prowess. Then they won an invitation to offer their resignations to Porterdale's City Manager. Officer Dale accepted the fabulous prize and tendered her resignation. Officer Chip refused and got the lovely consolation prize of being fired instead. This was not a blindingly smart move on the part of Chip, because now that he was fired as a cop, he might find it a tad difficult to find future employment as a cop.

Bet the two of them didn't expect *that* outcome from their little wager.

Source: Associated Press, CBS News

WHAT WOULD YOU DO
FOR VANILLA ROAST?

We **know you love a quiz,** so here's one for you. You're
visiting a good friend when you notice that her neighbor has some truly excellent vanilla roast coffee and hazelnut
creamer while your friend does not. You want some coffee.
You need some coffee. What do you do?

1. Go up to your friend's neighbor and say: "Hi, I've got a
    serious coffee jones at the moment, and I was wonder-
    ing if you might be able to spare some of your right-
    eous vanilla roast. I'll be your *friend*."

2. Break into the guy's apartment to steal just enough
    coffee to get you through your caffeine shakes. Take
    some creamer, too. Repeat your breaking and entering
    whenever you need some more.

The first of these is the correct answer. We admit that it
makes you come across as a little *needy,* but it's better than
coming across as felonious, which is how "Brooks" appeared
when he performed this very same maneuver while visiting a
friend in the small town of North Pole, Alaska (which is, we
should note, not actually *at* the North Pole, although it is
close enough for most people).

Brooks apparently saw nothing wrong about a little breaking and entering into his friend's neighbor's apartment for
his coffee and cream. Of course, the neighbor (let's call him
"Alan") felt differently; no one likes home invasions, even if
all that's being taken is a hot beverage. After Brooks's friend

mentioned that she smelled coffee in her apartment and she knew she didn't have any, Alan decided to set-up a video camera to catch his coffee thief. Sure enough, there was Brooks, breaking in with a butter knife for his vanilla hazelnut treat.

Alan later told the local newspaper that if Brooks had just asked, he'd given him some coffee for free. But as it was, Brooks was arrested for burglary and tossed in the slammer. He's probably not going to get vanilla roast with hazelnut creamer in there.

Source: Associated Press

OH, DEER

Here's an interesting fact for all of us who don't go out of our way to hunt down and kill woodland animals whose only crime was to be born tasty: in the state of Minnesota, you can hunt game with a gun, but it's illegal to hunt wild game with walkie-talkies. See, Minnesota believes that letting hunters have walkie-talkies to communicate and coordinate with each other during the hunt isn't fair to the game animals. (This brings up the interesting question of how, if walkie-talkies are unfair, then how are projectile weapons fair to animals exactly?) The point is: walkie-talkies and radios, you can't use 'em when you're in the mood for bangin' away at Minnesota wildlife.

If anyone should know about this little rule, it's Babe Winkelman, noted outdoorsman TV host and syndicated columnist. So it was probably a bit embarrassing for Winkelman when he was cited on his Minnesota property in the fall of 2003 for "unlawfully taking game with the use of a radio." Apparently an officer of Minnesota's Department of Natural Resources got a tip that hunters were using walkie-talkies, and decided to monitor radio traffic. That's when he caught Winkelman, his wife Kris, and another hunter chatting merrily away. See, that's the problem with radio frequencies; anyone can just listen in. Stupid walkie-talkies.

Winkelman contended that he was just using the walkie-talkies to keep in touch with the members of his large hunting group. But as part of the conversation the officer heard had Winkelman saying he was off to wake up a bunch of deer, followed by his wife saying that she was in her hunting stand "loaded, and ready to go," he wasn't buying that particular rationalization.

Time in the big house for this outdoorsy celebrity? Nope: Winkelman entered an "Alford plea," which is what you do if you want to say you're not guilty, yet reluctantly admit that if you were tried in front of a jury they'd probably beg to differ. As part of his plea agreement, Winkelman paid a fine and wrote about hunting ethics in his columns; if he can keep from doing something like that again for a year, his legal slate will be wiped clean. No doubt deer all over Minnesota are breathing easier after this decision. Now if they could just figure out a way to get those hunters to ditch those totally unfair *rifles*.

Source: Associated Press, *Minneapolis Star-Tribune,* NodakOutdoors.com

FLASHY STUPIDITY

We love the digital camera revolution as much as anybody. Nothing makes us happier than not having to shoot a whole roll of film and then pay for developing before we can see that we've taken yet another picture in which we've lopped off someone's head. Now we can see our bad photography instantaneously—and delete it before anyone else finds out.

Still, there's a dark side to the digital revolution, which is that the decreasing size and increasing ubiquity of digital cameras are encouraging the pervs out there to snap more creepy little pictures than ever before. The only good news about *that* is that while they're making cameras smaller, they're not making the perverts any smarter. This is especially the case with pervs in public, who are not smart enough to realize that public displays of stupidity call attention to themselves and also the attention of the cops.

As one did at the Roosevelt Field Mall in Garden City, New York, when "Sam" decided to devote a day to "upskirting"—a charming little practice that involves slipping a digital camera under a woman's skirt and photographing what you find there. Sam apparently had already had a busy day of photography when he slipped his camera under the miniskirt of a woman as she traveled up an escalator. The woman was apparently unaware that this creep was photographing her, probably because she didn't have eyes in back of her head.

Alas, poor Sam. Neither did he. Because if he had, he might have seen that the two men who stepped on to the escalator behind him were cops, who quickly discovered what

Sam was up to. It was the flash that gave him away. Stupid, stupid Sam. Sam was nabbed as soon as he got off the escalator; the cops checked the camera for photos. For Sam, the instant gratification that digital cameras can provide also immediately provided instamatic proof of his felonious photos. He was charged with unlawful surveillance, which carries a maximum sentence of four years in the slammer.

Not many opportunities for "upskirting" there, Sam. And if there are, it's probably best not to take a picture.

Source: *New York Newsday, New York Post*

Dim Bulbs in Bright Lights
ZOOLANDER (2001)

Our Dumb Guy: Derek Zoolander (Ben Stiller)

Our Story: Male Supermodel Derek Zoolander, depressed that he's lost the coveted best male model fashion award to up-and-coming Hansel (Owen Wilson), takes a gig as the head model for a sleazy clothes designer (Will Ferrell). Little does he know—or could he understand—that in doing so he's being primed to assassinate the Prime Minister of Malaysia, *Manchurian Candidate* style.

Dumb or Stoned? You can't hate him because he's beautiful, but you can pity him because he's stupid and certainly no on drugs. Zoolander may be pretty, but he is also pretty dumb.

High Point of Low Comedy: Zoolander and Hansel are confounded by how to get files out of a computer, so they start hitting it and grunting in frustration. As they do so, the theme music from *2001: A Space Odyssey* flares up in the background.

And Now, In His Own Words: Zoolander delivers the "eugoogaly" after his roomates' tragic deaths: "If there is anything that this horrible tragedy can teach us, it's that a male model's life is a precious, precious commodity. Just because we have chiseled abs and stunning features, it doesn't mean that we too can't not die in a freak gasoline fight accident."

He's Dumb, But Is the Film Good? Eh. It's not as bad as it could have been—male models? The fashion industry? All in all, it does a good job of poking fun at the really, really good-looking who are really, really not thinking.

CHAPTER 10

MOROHS AND
MOTOR VEHICLES

Ever notice how, the moment you get behind the wheel, other drivers' IQs drop about 50 points? We didn't really have a difficult time filling up this chapter with stories of automotive imbecility, which was just plain scary. Heck, we weren't sure we wanted to drive again when faced with the misadventures of intelligence-challenged on the highways and byways of this great big world. So for you, we offer a mere taste, just enough to remind you to be careful out there on the road.

ON THE ROAD,
DON'T LOOK AT THESE CURVES

Watching TV while driving is bad enough, but, please, we implore you: don't watch porn while driving your car. Driving is har ... er ... *difficult* enough when you're *not* distracted by a small screen filled with "adult entertainment." Not only are you distracting yourself, there's a good chance that you're distracting others on the road. As everyone knows, catching an animated flick or a *Barney* episode is easy enough to do through a moving minivan window since you can totally see what's on the screen from three lanes over. Purple dinosaurs are one thing, but pornography is a horse of a different color altogether, and one that certainly grabs a lot of adult attention.

If appeals to your sense of safety or decency don't move you, try this: if you watch porn in your car, you'll get a trip to the pokey. Such was the fate of "Derek," a Schenectady, New York, resident whose tricked-out Mercedes Benz included three DVD screens full of pure, X-rated viewing. As Derek tooled around the greater Schenectady area on this particular day, his in-car movie of choice was the somewhat disturbingly named *Chocolate Foam,* starring Pebbles, famous for her star turns in *Lewd Conduct #6* and *Ebony Extreme: Kitten.*

While Derek was stopped at a red light, he was so engrossed in Pebbles's Bam-Bam, as it were, that he didn't notice that behind his car was an unmarked police vehicle. And you say, well, it *was* unmarked. Fair enough. But even giving Derek that one, the Schenectady Police Department building, located at that very corner, *should not* have been difficult to miss. But we guess it wasn't.

Derek was pulled over to be cited for playing porn in his car, which is—who knew?—illegal in New York state; the law makes it a no-no to both watch TV while driving and publicly display "adult" material. Derek then compounded the problem by giving the policemen a false name when he went to get fingerprinted, possibly because he was also driving around with a suspended license. So on top of his charge of these other two charges, he also got slapped with a forgery charge. Oh, *Derek*.

Source: WNYT-TV, *New York Daily News*

VEHICULAR STUPIDITY, CANADIAN STYLE

Americans have this image of Canadians as a sensible **people,** but it turns out that they too have a vast potential for incredibly stupid acts. As evidence of this, allow us to present to you a compilation of vehicular stupidity from the Great White North, from just one province (Ontario) over just one weekend in 2004, as noted by the Ontario Provincial Police. These Canadians, at the very least, are not terribly sensible.

1. One 24-year-old driver was clocked doing 150 kph (93 mph); when he was pulled over, he explained that he was terrified of the freeways and was speeding so he could get off of it faster.

2. Another sterling excuse for speeding, from a 27-year-old: "I'm running out of gas and I wanted to get to the gas station fast." (And now, the science: to drive faster increases air turbulence around your car, increasing drag—and lowering your gas mileage. Dope.)

3. One car was stopped because the windshield was taped to the car. That's worth a trip on the back of a tow truck.

4. Our personal award for stupidest Canadian driver goes to the guy who not only neglected to wear a seatbelt (dumb) but also didn't bother to strap down the four children in the car with him (criminally idiotic); one of the kids was holding the driver's bucket seat steady because the seat was completely broken (just plain

sad). The car was towed and the driver got slapped with five moving violations, one for each unseatbelted human.

5. A close second: a fellow, who had been waved over for a babyseat inspection, tried to switch seats with the passenger before the cops came over. Not that it mattered, since both the guy and his female passenger had suspended licenses. But wait, there's more! The driver also had no insurance, the car's plates were stolen, and the driver was wanted on multiple warrants. And to top it all off, there was a court order forbidding him to come within 100 meters of his passenger. Car towed; woman and baby to a shelter; man to the slammer.

Source: *The Star* (Toronto)

DRIVING TOWARD TROUBLE

There's never a good time to display road rage. But some times *are* worse than others. One of the worst would be when you're in front of policemen, while you're out on bail, and there's an illegal substance in your car.

Certainly "Adam" didn't think this perfect storm of circumstances required him to play it cool. When he came storming out of his Florida house to rev up his Honda Accord, it didn't bother him in the slightest that there were ten uniformed deputies of the Palm Beach County Sheriff's office participating in a community event. In fact, Adam blasted down his street at high speeds, actually aiming at the cops, who quite naturally signaled to Adam to pull over. Instead Adam yelled at the cops to get out of his way, and phrased that request using language one typically would not impart to someone wearing a badge.

A couple of the sheriff's deputies got into their own cars and caught up with Adam, at which point there ensued a veritable festival of ticket-writing. And during this festival, the cops just happened to notice a coffee can in Adam's car, which just happened to contain about 20 grams of cocaine. And that's not just a moving violation, friends: That's possession with intent to sell.

And for the kicker: Adam was already out on bond for another completely unrelated charge, but seeing as he lacked the wisdom *not* to antagonize the cops or traffic in coke, he was placed in the cooler without the opportunity to spring himself once more. This is what road rage gets you, especially when it's so poorly timed.

Source: WESH.com, Associated Press

I WASN'T SPEEDING. THE EARTH JUST ROTATED SLOWER

Grab a pencil: It's time for a quiz! According to Australia's *Herald Sun* newspaper, which of the following are actual excuses given by people caught violating the law in their wheeled vehicles:

1. "A red light means *stop*? You know, I never knew that before."

2. "I would have put on the brakes, but my cat was asleep on my lap and I didn't want to disturb him."

3. "I just wanted to see if my speedometer is accurate when I go *really fast*."

4. "I was in a hurry to get home. My dog's having an epileptic fit."

5. "I'm not wearing a seatbelt because I have a broken arm."

6. "I was driving my motorbike at 200 kilometers an hour (124 mph) because the sun is setting and it's dangerous to drive a motorcycle at night."

Which ones are real excuses? They *all* are. They're just not real good excuses. Drive carefully, now. And remember, red means stop.

Source: *Herald Sun* (Australia)

THE WRONG FAKE ID

You know, there are a lot of really excellent reasons not to use a fake ID. And here's another!

Meet "Jim." Jim was zooming down the road near Lafayette, Indiana, when he was pulled over by a state trooper for speeding. Now, at this point we don't know why Jim decided it would be a prudent course of action to present the state trooper with a fake ID, although if we had to guess, we would figure because that way the ticket would be written to someone else, and Jim could continue his speedy ways unencumbered by points on his actual license. So up comes the officer, and out comes the fake ID. It's a good plan.

Except for the small detail that the fake ID is from a real person. And that real person is wanted in Texas for attempted murder, a more serious charge to have on one's record than speeding. Jim gets a free trip to jail, and after he presents proof of his true identity, he is also charged with identity deception and false informing, the first of which can get you three years in prison (we also suspect the original speeding violation was transferred over to Jim's real name. The Indiana State Police are just helpful that way).

The moral to the story is to just show your real ID. Or at the very least, don't show an ID that has a thicker police file than you do. In that case it's the crime you *didn't* commit that's going to get you in trouble.

Source: Associated Press

A SHORT CUT,
OR A LONG WAY DOWN?

We've all lost our car in a mall parking lot: You park, go shopping, and the next thing you know it's six hours later and you can hardly remember what section of the parking garage your car is in. Then you wander aimlessly and wonder how you'll ever get home. So when you *do* find your car, you want to run to it as quickly as you can, like a lost love, and then never return to the mall again, or at least until the next time you want a corn dog or need a killer pair of shoes.

That being that case, we understand how "Gladys" felt when, after wandering though an Orlando, Florida, mall's garage, she spotted her car—only it was one building over from where she stood. The safest way to get to her car was to go back into the mall and find the exit that led to the garage where her car was waiting for her. This whole process would have taken several minutes. But instead, Gladys was so anxious to reunite with her vehicle that she decided to just leap the two-and-a-half-foot space that separated the car garages to reach her car in a matter of seconds.

One small detail was overlooked; while the gap between the parking garages was about two-and-a-half-feet wide, the parking garage was *also* about six stories up. So when Gladys didn't quite make the leap across, she made the plunge down. Way down. All the way down to the concrete six stories below her.

The good news is that she lived. The bad news is that the shortcut ended up costing her a lot more than lost time.

Source: WESH.com

A CRUSHING LOSS

Now, we realize that y'all don't come to a book called the *Book of the Dumb* for helpful public service announcements, but on the other hand we don't want you doing something stupid if it can be avoided. As much as we like writing about people doing dumb things, we don't want any of you, our fine readers, to show up in the book unintentionally. So here's our small piece of advice for you today:

> If you lose something in a trash Dumpster, make sure it's not pick-up day before you go digging in it.

It seems a simple lesson, but was lost on "Irene," a woman who lost her keys in the Dumpster outside her Ridgeland, Mississippi, apartment complex. Irene needed her keys—who doesn't? So in she went, sifting through the trash so she could get on with the rest of her life. We guess either she didn't realize the trash guys were coming that day, or simply assumed that she could get out in time—or that the garbage guys would look in to see if there were any actual live people in the Dumpster before they emptied it. Whatever Irene's reasoning was, it turned out to be faulty. The trash guys showed up, speared the dumpster with that forklift-like attachment, and tossed its contents into the trash truck, with Irene along for the ride.

A stinky situation—but also a life-threatening one for Irene, since after the dumpster's contents ended up in the garbage truck, the truck's driver started compacting the trash, which would have made things a very tight squeeze for Irene. Fortunately for Irene, people heard her screaming from the back of the truck and told the driver to stop. Irene was pulled out of the mess and taken to a nearby hospital for pains in several of her joints. No kidding. No word if she actually ever found her keys.

David Myhan, a district manager for Waste Management, whose Dumpster it was, suggests that people who have lost something in the garbage call the company, who will dispatch someone to root through the garbage for you, which will keep you from getting dirty and/or compacted into a square shape. "We take this real seriously," he said, to a local newspaper. "We do not want people getting in our containers." Leave the trash-digging to the professionals, folks.

Source: *The Clarion Ledger* (Jackson, MS)

SHE CAN PARK THERE FOR 17 YEARS

Let's say you've been given a 100-year-old gold coin worth $1,000, because, oh, it was "$1000 century-old coin day" at the local minor league ball park. What you should do next is take that coin home, lovingly encase it in plastic or a wall safe, and tell the children that if they so much as breathe on it that you'll ground them until they're eighteen. What you should not do is leave it around like so much loose change. Because if you do, you may do something stupid with it.

As did "Marta," from Paarl, South Africa. Seems that she inherited from her parents some very valuable gold sovereign coins, minted in 1890. She stored them rather lackadaisically, and they managed to get mixed in with a bunch of other coins. So one day she scoops up some coins, drives her car downtown, parks. and slips a coin into the parking meter. One of the 1890 coins worth $1,000. That's a *lot* of parking.

Her reaction, as reported in the Cape Argus newspaper: "I can't believe I could have done something like that." We bet the coin was surprised, too. But perhaps not as much as another one of the coins, which the woman suspected she spent as a 20-pence piece (which it apparently resembled), which would be worth, oh, a few pennies or so here in the States. The woman's excuse for mixing up her money: She was shopping without her glasses. Probably the last time she'll be doing that. The woman has asked town officials to be on the lookout for the coin. We're sure they were right on that.

Source: *Cape Argus* (South Africa), Reuters

THE CASE OF THE TOO CLEVER LICENSE PLATE

By definition, people who have vanity plates on their cars and motorcycles want to be noticed (they're not called humility plates, after all). Jim Cara of Delaware was no exception—he wanted to give people a chuckle when they read his motorbike plates, so he selected what he thought was a clever little statement: "NO TAG." Because, see, he had a tag, and the tag said "no tag!" It was, like, *totally* meta. And thus did Jim Cara of Delaware feel mightily pleased with himself.

Until, that is, he started receiving the traffic violations—more than 200 of them, ranging in offenses from speeding to meter violations, with fines from $55 to $125 (which would mean the total amount would have been at least eleven grand). Either someone had been borrowing Cara's wheels and flaunting the law on a very rapid basis or something had gone horribly wrong somewhere in the ticketing system.

It seems that when you have a license plate with the words "NO TAG," all the violations for cars that don't actually have plates suddenly get attributed to you, because police officers and meter maids alike write "no tag" on the violations. Because computers aren't smart enough to realize the clever little license plate joke, Cara's vehicle became the most heavily fined in the state. Cara became understandably twitchy about hitting the road on his motorbike. "I messed up the system so bad," Cara said. "I wonder if they can put me in jail or something?"

Good news for Cara—he got in touch with real live humans, who quickly realized what the problem was and fixed it, so the cops wouldn't throw him in the pokey for hundreds of violations he never incurred. Spokesmen at the Delaware Division of Motor Vehicles suggested that Cara change his plate, but he refused: "I want to keep it," he said. "I think it's awesome." At least until the next computer screw-up.

Source: Delaware Online

The Annals of Ill-Advised Television

TODAY'S EPISODE:
MY MOTHER THE CAR

Starring in this Episode: Jerry Van Dyke and Ann Sothern

Debut Episode: September 14, 1965, on NBC

The Pitch: It's just like *Mr. Ed,* except the talking horse is a talking car, female, and the main character's mom. An everyday guy (Jerry Van Dyke) is stunned to find that his dearly departed mother (Ann Sothern) has been reincarnated as a jalopy (a 1928 Porter—although in reality no such model exists). He buys the car and takes it home much to the consternation of his family (who wanted a station wagon), and to the envy of car collector Captain Manzini, who plots to get the car for his own just about every week.

It Seemed Like a Good Idea at the Time Because: TV networks were looking for kooky ideas in 1965, partly because of the success of *Bewitched* and *The Man From U.N.C.L.E.* the year before. Other TV shows from the class of '65 include *I Dream of Jeannie* and *The Smothers Brothers Show* (*not* the *Smothers Brothers Comedy Hour,* but a sitcom in which one of the brothers was a ghost). Given its contemporaries, a show about a car inhabited by some schlub's dead mother probably just seemed par for the course.

In Reality: The show was pilloried almost immediately for its profound stupidity, and critics were none to kind about its star, either: A review in *Time* noted that "Jerry Van Dyke . . . has finally answered the question, what is it that Jerry hasn't got that Brother Dick has?" The show also had the misfortune of competing against two adult-themed dramas on the other networks: *Rawhide* on CBS and *Combat* on ABC, although this had the interesting side effect of leaving the kid market to *Car*—which was enough to help this jalopy of a show wheeze through an entire full season.

How Long Did It Last? 30 episodes—more episodes than in today's TV seasons, and the most of any show in the Annals of Ill-Advised Television. The last episode ran April 5, 1966.

Were Those Responsible Punished? Not in the slightest. Show creators Allen Burns and Chris Hayward would go on to greater TV rewards: Burns would help create the *Mary Tyler Moore Show* as well produce spinoffs *Rhoda* and *Lou Grant*. Hayward became a producer on *Get Smart* and *Barney Miller*. Star Jerry Van Dyke, who had turned down *Gilligan's Island* to be in *Car*, would later find fame on the long-running '90s TV hit *Coach*. Ann Sothern went on to get an Oscar nomination for 1987's *The Whales of August*, 60 years after her first appearance in film. Sothern died in 2001 and to date has not been reincarnated as any sort of automobile.

CHAPTER 11

OUTSMARTED BY ANIMALS

There's dumb. There's *really* dumb. And then, a cut below that, there's the sort of dumb that even animals roll their eyes at. Yes, ladies and gentlemen, here and now, for your delight and edification, a series of incidents involving animals and humans, in which it is clear that the smartest living things in the stories are not the ones with the opposable thumbs.

CETTE PANTHÉRE EST TRÉS PETITE, NON?

Those French. Oh, stop your giggling. We haven't even told you what stupid thing they've done yet. Really, now. Let us do our work, here.

Where were we? Ah, yes, those French. We understand that France, having been occupied by humans for several thousands of years at least—humans who have a well-justified aversion to having large predators loping around where they live—might not have all that much going on in the way of lions and tiger and bears (oh my) these days. So when it was reported that several residents of Marseille had seen a large black panther roaming around, naturally everyone was a little on edge. Authorities shut down a large recreational area outside of town where the panther had been spotted—wouldn't do to have tourists eaten—and dozens of soldiers and police went through the area to find the large feline predator.

And they found it, sort of. What they found *was* a predator, and it *was* feline, but "large" was strictly a relative term. It was an ordinary if somewhat big-boned black housecat, which experts estimated being two feet long from tip to tail and weighing in at 22 pounds. For comparison, your average panther typically weighs in at 100 to 200 pounds and can be seven feet long, not including the tail. But we guess you *could* confuse a house cat with a panther. If you were a *gnome.*

We wonder how the good people of Marseille would describe a real panther. We're not sure, but just in case, we're instructing our clipping service to look out for stories with the words "Marseille" and "Saber-toothed Tiger."

Source: Reuters, www.iol.co.za

THE GREAT IMMOBILE OWL

In retrospect, it could be said—not by *polite* people, but even so—that the bird enthusiasts of Wrenthorpe, West Yorkshire, England had perhaps gotten a little smug. And why not? It *was* near their little village that storks only rarely found in Britain had been recently spotted. And so when a new, large, mysterious owl appeared in their midst, the birdwatchers were thrilled. It was just more proof that, if you were a bird or a birdwatcher, Wrenthorpe was a tidy English paradise.

What was nice about the owl was that it seemed to have a predictable routine. Every morning, there it was on a telegraph pole. Really, you could set your watch to it. And after a few days of *that*, well, some people got suspicious. As local bird enthusiast Harold Barrett mentioned to the local press, "Owls can stay in one place for a while, but not that long."

So eventually someone went to get a closer look at the owl. At which point it was discovered the owl was a decoy nailed to the pole. To scare off other birds or to fake out the now embarrassed and angry birdwatchers? The prankster has not been found to explain his motives, and the owl, of course, is silent.

Representatives of the Royal Society for the Protection of Birds offered these consoling words: "It is great that they are looking out for birds. Let's just hope that next time they spot something more than a decoy."

Source: Reuters

MEOW, BABY

If you were suddenly missing a finger, wouldn't you *mention* it to someone? Wouldn't you at least *acknowledge* it?

We ask because in May 2004, there was a spare finger lying outside the jaguar exhibit at the Rio Grande Zoo in Albuquerque, New Mexico, with no one around to claim it. It turned out to be a more complicated affair then just poking a finger in the cage. To get to the jaguar, the perp had to go past metal barriers and cactus, and avoid detection by the zoo staff to reach his quarry. Make no mistake, it took real initiative to lose this finger. So it was surprising that no one cared to claim it.

Be that as it may, the zoo staff had their suspicions as to who Mr. Nine Fingers was. Particularly, they had their eye on a frequent zoo patron who had been there nearly every day over the past few years and, more importantly, who was seen running from the zoo on the day the finger would have gone missing. Apparently, not only was he running, but he was doing so with his hand in his pocket and with a dark stain spread over his pants. He was a member of the zoo, so they looked up his number in their database and gave him a call. And he said something along the line of, well, I've got ten fingers, so you've got the wrong guy.

Well, he *didn't,* and they didn't. The mystery of the missing finger was solved pretty much like you'd expect. Back at some point when this zoo patron *did* have ten fingers, he'd been fingerprinted by the police. So the zoo handed over the gruesome jaguar treat to the police, who compared its fingerprint and matched it up with that of the zoo patron.

Confronted by the overwhelming evidence of the fingerprint-ing (and, one imagines, the uncomfortable fact of being able only to count to nine on his hands), the patron reluctantly admitted to the former ownership of said finger.

The zoo didn't press charges against the patron, reason-ing that having a finger snapped off by a predator is probably punishment enough. But they *did* ban him from the zoo, we guess just in case he hadn't learned his lesson. Well, look at it this way: if he doesn't learn it after another eight or nine times, we figure the problem will just take care of itself.

This is an object lesson to all you would-be animal lovers out there: just because you think you have a special relation-ship with an animal at the zoo, it doesn't mean that the ani-mal agrees. This is especially true of, say, animals who are at the top of their food chain in their native habitat and have a mouth full of teeth especially designed for shearing off body parts. But don't take *our* word for it, take the word of zoo director Ray Darnell, who told the press: "They're not your friends, they're not your pets. They're wild animals." Preach it, Ray.

Source: Associated Press, TheNewMexicoChannel.com

PSSST...DOGS DON'T GET REPRESENTATIONAL ART

First, let us note our enduring respect for the mail carriers of North America, who without fail deliver unto us all our bills, magazines, and circulars. Without you guys we wouldn't have anything to look forward to in the late morning to early afternoon hours of our workdays. You guys rock. And we also note that in doing your job, you are also often forced to deal with large, angry dogs. You have our sympathy, and our best wishes for accurate aim with that pepper spray you carry on your belt.

Having said that, we can't help but think that the folks at Canada Post were a wee bit oversensitive in the summer of 2004 when they lobbied the Canadian Pet Valu chain of pet stores to stop carrying a brand of doggie treats known as Bark Bars, on the rationale that these dog snacks come in two provocative shapes: cats, which Canada Post is neutral about, and mail carriers, which it is not. "I will tell you, personally, I think it was in very poor taste, considering the hazards that our carriers have out there every day," said Canada Post spokesperson John Caines.

This does seem to suggest that someone at Canada Post is under the impression that dogs will look at the snacks, which are vaguely human-shaped with the word "mail" stamped on them, then look at their owner's mail carrier (who despite his or her job, probably does not have the word "mail" stamped chest-wide) and see a one-to-one correlation. Which would suggest that the dogs could, you know, *read*. The wonders of the Canadian educational system notwithstanding, this seems a little much.

Nevertheless, the Pet Valu chain decided to pull the mail carrier-shaped treats, citing its own largely neglected guideline of not selling anything relating to mail shapes. The cat-shaped treats, however, are still a go, so look out, feline lovers.

Ironically, in the United States, mail carriers reportedly have a different relationship to the carrier-shaped snacks; they carry them around to feed to the dogs on their routes. Better the dogs chew on the snacks than on the actual mail carrier.

Source: *The Globe and Mail* (Toronto), Reuters

AND THEN THE ENTIRE
TOWN IMPLODED FROM THE
WEIGHT OF ALL THE PUNS

You have to understand that the previous city manager of Ridgefield, Washington, really was something of a washout. Apparently he tried to remove lead paint from the city hall without paying attention to environmental regulations. So while he did save the city $15,000 by ignoring the regulations, his penny-pinching also, according to court filings, released an "immense cloud of toxic dust" which had something like six times the acceptable level of lead. And then there were the lead paint chips flowing into the sewer and then in the nearby lake . . . in all, a real mess. The city manager was suspended and then fired and then faced charges of official misconduct.

So whom to elect as the city manager? The local citizenry decided that Otis, who keeps regular hours at Ridgefield Hardware, would be a fine candidate. He was well-known and well-liked around town—everyone called him by his first name, after all. He was known to be level-headed and not pushy, never interrupted people, and seemed to value people *as* people, not as just more votes. And everyone was positive that Otis would never do anything as damn foolish as try to strip lead paint illegally. In July 2004, fliers went up around town: Otis for City Manager, paid for by the "He Will Do Better Than the Last Guy Committee."

The one drawback: Otis was only 11 years old. But maybe that really wasn't such a drawback, because that meant that he was 77 in dog years, a more accurate reflection of his age since Otis, after all, was a dog, a Boston Terrier, to be exact. "A doggone improvement," read another sign, and you can just imagine all the rest of the dog puns that went from there. Oh, and of course, let's not miss this quote, from Otis's owner, Scott Hughes: "They wanted to know if there were any scandals in his background. I told them, no, he's been fixed."

Are the good people of Ridgefield completely out of their collective gourd? We suspect they're probably letting off steam, and that when push comes to shove, they'll elect an actual, live human (complicating matters was the emergence of Drumstick, a chicken, as a second candidate, possibly splitting the animal vote). But it does have us feeling just a little bit sorry for the previous city manager. It's one thing to be fired and face charges of official misconduct. It's another thing to have been so bad at your job that someone jokingly suggests a dog would be a better city manager than you . . . and the *entire city* agrees. Good luck getting that next position, pal. Although if Otis gets elected, there *will* be a open spot at the hardware store.

Source: Associated Press, *The Vancouver Columbian*

PLEASE, THINK
OF THE ST. BERNARDS

They say that breaking up is hard to do, but splitting the proceeds afterward can be just plain annoying. There are all the questions of who gets what, where it goes, and who pays for it all. It's enough to make you want to stay together to just avoid the organizational nightmare. Now people breaking up in Canada have a new wrinkle on the break-up proceedings: pet support.

It all started when the relationship ended: Ken Duncan of Warburg, Alberta, and Barbara Dawn Boschee put the brakes on their six-year-relationship, the accouterments of which included two St. Bernards: Mojo, adjudged to be "her" dog, and "Crunchy," who was "his" (the dogs, we'd bet, were neutral on the whole ownership question). Sadly for Duncan, he couldn't find an apartment that would allow him to keep a large, slobbery dog bred to rescue Alpine frostbite victims, so Crunchy stayed with Boschee, and Duncan agreed to pay for any extraordinary expenses regarding the dog.

That's not enough, said the judge presiding over the couple's spousal support settlement in June 2004. Henceforth, Duncan would have to pay $200 (that's Canadian dollars) a month for the upkeep of his dog—and retroactively spring for payments for the previous year. Boschee claimed that amount was fair, listing monthly expense of $55 for food and $30 for rug shampooing because Crunchy has "lots of accidents." Duncan—who agreed to pay—nevertheless maintained that he never spent more than $40 a month on dog food. The real irony, said Duncan: "I can't even visit my dog, 'cause the judge won't let me. I miss her a lot. I can't even watch a movie with a St. Bernard in it."

So beware, Canadian couples! Before you end that relationship, won't you please think of the pets? And the costs you'll have in supporting them.

Source: Canoe.ca

A BONER OF A REGULATION

Dogs are man's best friend (says so right there on the label), and what do they want from us? The odd scratch behind the ears, the occasional Frisbee throw, and yes, every once in a while it'd be nice if we threw our furry pal a bone. Word on the street is that they love those crunchy, marrow-packed treats, and hey, it's not like *you're* going to gnaw on it.

Well, the friendship might be strained in Europe, where EU bureaucrats have announced that no longer can butchers give their spare bones to dogs. If you're a butcher, and you debone a piece of meat, that bone is now defined as a "waste by-product" (as is any trimmed fat), and as waste by-product, it must be disposed of properly—it has to be incinerated. Give a dog a bone, and you can get fined for improperly disposing of waste.

What makes this regulation well and truly stupid is not that butchers can no longer give customers bones for their dogs; what makes it well and truly stupid is that they *can,* so long as everyone pretends that they're *not.* See, by EU regulations, if you take the bone out, it's a by-product and therefore must be incinerated—but, as a spokesman for Britain's Department for the Environment, Food, and Rural Affairs noted: "Customers can take bones when they buy deboned meat if it is for human consumption." So all you do is go into the butcher shop, declare your intention to personally jaw on a bone, take the bone home, and feed it to the dog. It's the carnivorous equivalent of "Don't Ask, Don't Tell."

We wonder if those EU bureaucrats have told their own dogs about their new "no bones" policy. And if so, how well they sleep at night. Dogs are simply domesticated wolves, you know. If you won't *give* them a bone, they may be inclined to *take* one.

Source: *The Sun* (UK)

IF YOU GIVE
A POLAR BEAR A COOKIE

We're not sure what it is with people being dumb in **zoos,** but this scenario seems to take the cake. There was drinking (of course). There was the blackout. There was the waking up in the zoo in Tallinn, Estonia; moreover, there was the waking up in the Tallinn Zoo in the polar bear exhibit. Okay? Got all the details? Holding them in your brain? Now, pay attention:

Don't try to give the polar bear a cookie.

Of course, put yourself in the place of "Ivan," who found himself in just the sticky pickle we described. Hungover, disoriented, and facing a massive predator, perhaps he thought that offering the sweet crispy treat will distract the animal long enough for him to run away. Or perhaps Ivan, brought up as so many of us have been on the idea of polar bears being cute spokes animals for fizzy beverages, thought they would bond over a doughy treat. But the fact is polar bears are carnivorous, wild animals—certainly not to be trifled with.

It was his screams that brought Ivan to the attention of the zoo staff, who found the polar bear busy chomping away, not the cookie, but the hand with which it was offered. They took Ivan to the hospital. Meanwhile Tallinn Zoo manager Mati Kaal, who has seen run-ins with the polar bear and dumb humans before, offered this blasé yet scary comment: "This is the first hand. In other cases it's been the whole arm." So maybe the cookie was a useful deterrent after all.

Source: iol.co.za

The Really Stupid Quiz

OUTSMARTED BY ANIMALS

One of the stories is a true animal tale, the other two are more made up than a Jackalope. You make the call.

1. There are many reasons not to attack a wasp's nest with a flame thrower made from a can of WD–40, and "Sid," of Painesville, Ohio, illustrates one of them. Sid's plan was to torch the wasp's nest that was residing in the bushes outside his home, but he neglected to consider that in lifting his lighter into the aerosol spray to ignite it, some of the spray might get onto his hand, thus catching his hand on fire. He then neglected to consider that as he was hopping around in pain over his burned hand, he might accidentally brush up against the wasp nest he planned to burn, thus enraging the residents of the nest, who would deploy in a swarm to sting Sid several dozen times before he could manage to retreat to his home to call 911. "Looking back, I could have handled it better," Sid admitted to a reporter, at the hospital.

2. In Waco, Texas, the owner of "Preston," an Australian Shepard mix, probably thought he was being clever when he trained his pup to retrieve beer cans, just like that dog does in that commercial. Unfortunately, the owner apparently did not teach his dog to distinguish between the owner's beers and the beers of others. Or perhaps he chose not to, because on a visit to Waco's Cameron Park, when Preston

began retrieving beers from other picnickers, his owner began drinking the ill-gained booty. This was good, beery fun until one of Preston's beer-snatch victims followed Preston to his master, identified himself as an off-duty Waco policeman, and arrested Preston's owner for receiving stolen property. Preston was not charged.

3. What would you call a rabbit with an explosive strapped to it? In this case, you'd call it Lucky. For one, that was its name. Second, when the two men taped that M-1000 explosive (the equivalent of a quarter stick of dynamite), lit the fuse, and then tossed the at-that-moment-ironically-named Lucky into Lake Don Castro in Castro Valley, California, they neglected to consider the fuse-quenching capacity of the lake. So Lucky was lucky that her tormentors weren't very smart. They were, however, arrested on misdemeanor charges of animal cruelty. This caused one of the men to complain, "I think that a lot of people are judging us without knowing us at all." When asked to explain why he strapped an explosive to a bunny, the man replied, "That's a real tough question to answer." We bet.

Answers on page 329.

Dim Bulbs in Bright Lights

BiLL & TED'S EXCELLENT ADVENTURE (1989)

Our Dumb Guys: Theodore "Ted" Logan (Keanu Reeves) and Bill S. Preston, Esq. (Alex Winter). And together, they are WYLD STALLYNS!!!!!

Our Story: Two mentally hypoxic teenagers from San Dimas, California, are about to flunk out of high school if they don't ace their history presentation. Lucky for them a mysterious stranger, Rufus (George Carlin), offers them the use of a time travel machine to do their most excellent research. They go back in time to procure august personages from the past, such as Abe Lincoln and Joan of Arc, to show how they would react to modern times.

Dumb or Stoned? We are supposed to believe that two hard rock-loving teenage wanna-bes who hang out in a convenience store parking lot in the late 1980s are *not,* in fact, stoned to the gills most of the time. Uh-huh. Whatever you say, guys.

High Point of Low Comedy: Bill and Ted convince Socrates (whose name they pronounce "So-crates") to go with them by quoting lines from rock band Kansas's 1970s hit "Dust in the Wind."

And Now, In Their Own Words: Ted, introducing Genghis Khan: "This is a dude who, 700 years ago, totally ravaged China, and who we were told, 2 hours ago, totally ravaged Ashman's Sporting Goods."

They're Dumb, But Is the Film Good? Not *really,* but for a film about stupid teenagers, it's surprisingly not gross or drugged-up. In its own dim-bulb way suggests that there might be something to that whole "education" thing teenagers may have heard about. And it's packed with one-liners that teenagers quoted to each other well into the 1990s. Still, be excellent to each other, dudes.

CHAPTER 12

POLITICAL PINHEADS

Ultimately, politics is about people; and as you'll learn in this chapter, it's often about dumb people. Let us note, however, that politically speaking, dumbness is an equal opportunity employer. In a way, it's nice to see stupidity evenly distributed across the entire political experience. In another way, it can make you want to hide in the basement stocked with a good supply of water and canned goods, just in case the political system implodes. Which way you're leaning can depend on what day it is and how many stories you read from this chapter. Courage.

SPELLING LESSON

Give New York City Councilwoman Margarita Lopez **this much credit:** her intentions were good, but she lost points on execution. Wanting to call attention to what she believed were deficiencies in educational policy, Lopez issued a press release attacking the policies of promoted by New York mayor Michael Bloomberg. There was just one thing Ms. Lopez forgot: when blasting someone else's educational policies, make sure that you yourself appear somewhat educated.

The misstep? See if you can spot it: "Why is Mayor Bloomberg and Chancellor Klein ignoring the fact that the test is flawed and discriminatory?" Okay, who can spot the grammatical error? Hands please, let's not have everyone shout it out at once. Yes, that's correct, the first "is" should be "are" in that sentence (there *are* two people referred to in the sentence).

Undaunted, Lopez's office shot out a second release asking: "Why are advocates targeted for examining testing **prodecures** and policies implemented by the Department of Education?" An excellent question, although it would have been made even *more* excellent through the simple use of a spell check. Lopez's office immediately moved to correct the error by issuing a revised press release. The good news: "procedures" was no longer spelled "prodecures." The bad news: it wasn't spelled "procedures," either—instead, we were introduced to "proceedures." Thus was the point of Lopez's press release lost in the din of giggling about her staff's inability to wield the language in a competent fashion.

Lopez herself did not write the press releases, but nevertheless she took the heat, proclaiming: "I take total responsibility . . . The member of my office who committed the mistake is going to be protected by me, the same the way that I protect the children of the City of New York." Hopefully she'll hold the children of the City of New York to higher spelling standards.

Source: *New York Post*

NOT CLEAR ON THE "HAVE TO WIN PEOPLE'S VOTES" THING

The spring of 2004 wasn't the most congenial time in American politics, what with the snowballing presidential campaign and some particularly bad moments in Iraq splitting the nation into highly partisan and largely annoying camps. But even in moments of high political duress, it's a good idea to keep one's cool. It's not like the 1850s, when members of Congress could whack each other with their canes, or even the 1950s, when Harry Truman threatened to beat the crap out of a newspaper critic who had given his daughter a bad review. This is the twenty-first century, and we try to be a little more genteel.

Perhaps Democratic Representative Pete Stark from California didn't get the memo, because when one of his constituents sent him a fax complaining about his vote on a resolution he lost his cool. The constituent, a member of the National Guard and a law student, wrote, in part: "Your no vote on this resolution is a disgrace to the people of this district who have elected you . . . I urge you to stop your contemptuous display of bitter partisanship."

Less than an hour later, a message appeared on the constituent's cell phone. It was from Congressman Stark himself. He basically ripped the guy a new one, suggesting that "you don't know what you're talking about," and that "I doubt if you could spell half the words in the letter, and somebody wrote it for you." However, he promised to call back later "and let you tell me more about why you think you're such a great [profanity deleted] hero." Clearly, Stark wasn't worried about getting this guy's vote in November.

Sure, it sounds like Stark got the better of the guy. Here's a tip to you future leaders of America, however: if you leave a message spouting bile upon one of your constituents on his cell phone, don't be surprised if he doesn't keep it to himself. Not long after Stark left the message, a tape of it was aired on Rush Limbaugh's radio show, which allowed that famously bloviating talk show host several minutes of his patented liberal bashing. Probably not what Stark would have wanted at all.

Source: NBC11.com, Trivalleyherald.com

PUT DOWN THAT COMIC BOOK!

Here's a little story to inspire confidence in your political institutions. Over there in Japan, prime minister Junichiro Koizumi had a little sit down with the newest members of parliament from his party and asked them do something for him—stop reading comic books at work!

Is this the Japanese parliament or a high school? If it were the latter, that might explain a lot about Japan's anemic economic performance the last several years. But in fact it's the former. The lawmakers are reading comic books because in Japan, comic books (or "manga") aren't just for kids; they're common reading material for average adults (it helps that many of the comic books in Japan are quite, uh, *racy* compared to what most American comic books). Everybody has their favorite manga—even parliamentarians.

And therein lay the problem for Prime Minister Koizumi. As newer members of the parliament are seated in the front, the prime minister was getting a mighty fine view of the boys goofing off. So down came the heel. "Don't . . . read comic books in Parliament while in session," Koizumi was quoted in the Japanese press as saying. "You can be seen very clearly from the prime minister's seat. You should really stop that—it's disgraceful."

And if they don't stop, Koizumi is going to give them detention.

Source: Associated Press

WELL, THEN, STOP PRINTING THEM WITH FLAVORED INK

We can't say enough good things about Canada, who even the most jingoistic American will admit is a perfect neighbor. Be that as it may, every once in a while we get an indication that up there in the Great White North, they do things a little differently.

As an example, take the following bit of advice, from the Web site of Elections Canada: "Eating a ballot, not returning it or otherwise destroying or defacing it constitutes a serious breach of the Canada Elections Act." Which led us to ask, in that logical way of ours, well, *have* Canadians been eating their ballots in numbers large enough to warrant a warning on a government Web site? Sure, you'll always have one or two odd ducks who'll snack on a ballot just because they're pathological paper eaters, but to have the government actually address the issue, there's got to be a bunch of Canadians looking for snacks at their ballot box.

The answer is that indeed there are. The Edible Ballot Society of Canada promotes ballot ingestion as a form of civil disobedience: "Voting is not only useless, it actually undermines genuine democracy by legitimizing an inherently undemocratic process . . . Check out great dishes such as The Ballot Burger, with a side order of Campaign Literature. Or perhaps you enjoy cheese and would like to try a Ballot Fondue," says the group's Web site (everyone has a Web site these days).

The EBS notes that members of its pulp-loving crew were arrested for eating their ballots in the 1997 and 2000 elections; apparently these incidents caused enough consternation for Elections Canada that they posted a warning. It must have worked, since Canada's 2004 national election was by all indications free of ballot ingestion. We guess this time around, the ballot choices were more palatable than the ballots themselves.

We wonder if the movement would ever catch on here in the United States, although most Americans, confronted with the choices on their ballots are probably less inclined to chuck their ballots *down* their throats than the opposite maneuver entirely.

Source: Reuters, The Edible Ballot Society

VICE PRESIDENTIAL MISPRINT

Newspapers can be a rough gig, especially in New York City, where three daily newspapers kick and bite and scratch and gouge at each other trying to get to the stories first (well, the *Post* and the *Daily News* scratch and gouge; the *Times* sends out a manservant to rough up the others). So in early July 2004, when it was time to sniff out which person Democratic presidential candidate John Kerry would choose as his running mate, all three newspapers were hot on the trail.

And it was the scrappy, sassy *New York Post*—a frequent source for this very book!—that pulled out the scoop: "Kerry's Choice: Dem picks Gephardt as VP candidate," blasted the *Post* from its front page, referring to Missouri congressman Richard Gephardt. "Gephardt—a 63-year-old power player in Washington for nearly three decades—beat out such contenders as Sen. John Edwards of North Carolina," read the story, which led on the front and then booted to page four, which was filled with colorful pictures of the erstwhile VP candidate. In all, a nice presentation of a nice scoop—and the *Post* had it in the newsstands while the other papers were still speculating on Kerry's selection.

There was one *minor* factual error with the scoop, however: mainly, that Kerry selected John Edwards for his VP candidate, not Gephardt. So by 9 a.m., the *Post's* big scoop turned into one of the great screw-ups in New York newspaper history and in political reporting—not quite supplanting the *Chicago Tribune's* infamous "Dewey Defeats Truman" headline, but rather comfortably settling in to position number two.

Were the other media outlets understanding of the *Post's* error? Nope. The *New York Daily News* was particularly gleeful: "In another of its 'Dewey Defeats Truman'–style 'exclusives,' The *New York Post* reported on its front page and website Tuesday that Missouri Rep. Gephardt was Kerry's choice," the competing tabloid crowed. "The struggling tabloid's site pulled the embarrassing image of its flat-out-wrong front page and swapped in a wire story instead of its sure-to-stay-exclusive original, but thousands of copies of the baffling Gephardt front page were already on the streets."

Meanwhile, over at media industry bible *Editor & Publisher,* things weren't much nicer: "*The New York Post* . . . became an object of ridicule Tuesday morning," E&P noted on the same day. *The Post,* which posts its front page on its Web site, pulled down the page and replaced it with its back page; the "scoop" article was also pulled down. Rather sadly, however, there were still all those thousands of physical copies of the newspaper out there, which were rapidly snapped up as collector's items: "Copies of the paper are already available on eBay," the E&P said. Some wags speculated that the *Post* purposefully ran the wrong story simply to get a sales spike.

All that was left was for *Post* Editor-in-Chief Col Allan to grovel. "We unreservedly apologize to our readers for the mistake," Allan wrote in a statement, which did not otherwise explain how such a monumental flub could have happened at one of America's largest dailies. Later rumors suggested it was the owner of the *Post,* Rupert Murdoch, who passed along the information (and who was going to disagree with *him*?)

Oh, well. As they saying goes, "Today's news is tomorrow's fishwrap." And in this case the *Post* has the advantage that the story already stunk.

Source: *Editor & Publisher,* Associated Press,
New York Daily News, New York Post

The Annals of Ill-Advised Television

TODAY'S EPISODE: THE CHEVY CHASE SHOW

Starring in this Episode: Chevy Chase hosting his own talk show.

Debut Episode: September 7, 1993, on Fox

The Pitch: Pretty Simple: Comedian Chevy Chase turns into a talk show host and interviews other famous people and then does comedy bits, sort of like he did on that other late night show he did, what was it called? Oh yeah, *Saturday Night Live.*

It Seemed Like a Good Idea at the Time Because: Back in 1993, people were still laboring under the impression that Chevy Chase was amusing and might be worth watching for an hour a night. Also, the early '90s were a time when late night talks shows were undergoing upheavals—Jay Leno replacing Johnny Carson, David Letterman going into direct competition with the venerable *Tonight Show,* and unknown Conan O'Brien squatting in Letterman's old digs. If there was ever a time for the Fox network to throw a late night talk show into the mix, this was going to be it.

In Reality: Chase, who was relaxed and goofy enough on SNL, started *The Chevy Chase Show* with a flop-sweat, deer-in-the-headlights look of transfixed terror—a look that would stay with him during the entire run of the show. Chase's interview skills were remedial, and, aside from a fake news report (a leftover from his SNL days), his comedy bits were painfully unfunny. Fox, which had invested millions in the show and even renamed the theater the show took place in as "The Chevy Chase Theater" had a monumental turkey on its hands. "Chase's show became eerily fascinating to watch once the specter of Totally Lost Cause took over," *Washington Post* critic Tom Shales noted, after the show was mercifully canceled.

How Long Did It Last? Six weeks, which by most estimates was five weeks and four days too long.

Were Those Responsible Punished? Eh. Chase went back to work as a film star, kicking out progressively more mediocre efforts through the '90s and '00s (*Cops and Robbersons, Vegas Vacation, Snow Day*). However, he's still Chevy Chase, and you're not.

CHAPTER 13

ROMANCING
THE STONED

Despite all the public service announcements, some people continue to just say, "yes," which is why we suppose this next chapter exists. Full of tales of self-inflicted wounds from the drug wars, the following stories are great examples of the perils of unclean living. So stay away from the drugs or run a reasonably good chance of showing up in a future edition of this book. We think that's enough motivation for anyone.

WHEN NOT TO CALL THE POLICE

It all started when "Eddie" notified the Payson, Arizona, **police** that he'd been robbed and thieves had taken his bag. There he was at a gas station, minding his own business, when all of a sudden he'd been pushed to the ground and robbed. Eddie was quite naturally worried about his bag.

Well, the good news was that the bag was found—another person found it in the nearby Safeway parking lot. For reasons of natural curiosity, and possibly to determine the identity of the owner, our good Samaritan opened the bag to see what was inside. He didn't find any personal identification, but he *did* find something else of passing interest: about $5,000 worth of methamphetamine. At which point our Samaritan thought that maybe the police might be interested in this little bag.

And, of course, they were. Once they had it in their possession, they brought in Eddie, who identified it as his bag. To which the police said, more or less, well, okay—and is the 100 grams of crank in the bag *also* yours? To which Eddie said something like "Oh, *that*. That's not *mine*. I was just *holding* it."

Well, seems the police have a term for holding someone else's drugs; it's called *possession*. Which is what they charged Eddie with, as well as possession of drug paraphernalia. But what about the robbery? It turns out that it didn't happen—Eddie's bag wasn't stolen, he had just dropped it. We guess Eddie thought that if he reported it as stolen, the police would move on it quicker, and might not think to ask what was inside the bag. He was right about one of those.

Source: *The Payson RoundUp*

WHAT IF YOU GAVE A PARTY
AND NOBODY CAME, DUDE?

Here's a funny thing about people who are enthusiastic about marijuana: they sure like to *talk* about it a lot. Just ask them—and then try to get them to shut up. But when it comes time for action, they can be a bit lackadaisical. This may have something to do with their favorite herb, which does not exactly inspire a frenzied burst of activity; indeed, if it inspires any activity at all, it's usually 25 to 30 minutes of plucking at the same note on an out-of-tune guitar followed by the deeply introspective ingestion of two-thirds of a bag of Cheetos, followed by a nap.

Nevertheless, when British cannabis enthusiasts planned a festival of appreciation of and for Mary Jane at a park in Birmingham, police were on hand to handle the crowds. In Great Britain, pot has been downgraded to a Class C drug, which effectively means that you're no longer an automatic candidate for arrest. The police may look upon you with extreme disapproval and sniff haughtily at your knitted cap and Hacky Sack, but they won't arrest you. You would think this would encourage people to come out and celebrate their favorite smokable.

But let's remember that cannabis makes you mellow. *Really* mellow. Which may be why the attendance at the 2004 Birmingham cannabis festival was just one guy named Mark, who had come up from Chester. Not even the *organizers* showed up. The one guy who did show up noted to the BBC: "Cannabis users aren't the fastest starters, are they?" Apparently not. Maybe someone should have offered free Cheetos.

Source: BBC

NOT TOO SUBTLE

Whipping up highly illegal drugs is usually an activity that most people try to hide. If the local police take an interest in your activities, it's unlikely that you'll turn a profit and avoid jail time.

This is why we're puzzled at the tactics of "Jed," an alleged methamphetamine producer from Sarpy County, Nebraska. Jed wasn't actually out on the lawn, stirring up batches of meth, but he did something pretty close. He parked a 9,600 gallon tank of anhydrous ammonia out in front of his house, and snaked a hose from the tank into the house.

In addition to being very suspicious—anhydrous ammonia is used to make fertilizer, methamphetamines, and explosives—this substance is very dangerous. Spill a little bit of the stuff and you run the risk of caustic burns to your skin, eyes and other body tissue; breathe it in and you'll suffocate in relatively short order. No matter what you're up to with it, law enforcement is going to take a keen interest in the fact you have *a lot* of it around. So Jed's prominent ammonia display is certainly one of the dumbest things he could have done if he was trying not to get caught.

Jed's dumbness rewarded him with being hauled away on charges of meth possession and intent to sell, as well as possession of anhydrous ammonia, which was hauled away by a hazmat crew. Let's hope everyone in the neighborhood is breathing just a little bit easier.

Source: TheOmahaChannel.com

SMUGGLER'S BLUES

We don't pretend to be experts in the practice of smuggling drugs (and our mothers are grateful), but we hear things. And one of the things we hear is that there really is no good place on your body to smuggle them. Those customs people, they're not afraid to investigate in places you'd prefer they didn't. This was lost on "Brad," who had it in his mind to smuggle 1.2 kilos of cocaine into Australia. His super-magnificent plan to elude the customs people and the drug-sniffing dogs: he'd hide that two and a half pounds of coke in his underwear.

Now, let's think about this. First, we're pretty sure that to pull this off, you'd have to wear briefs, because boxers are just a little too loose for this kind of transport work. Second: what sort of idiot thinks 1.2 kilos of powdered substance in your tighty whities *isn't* going to be noticeable? Try this at home: go to your pantry and take out two and a half pounds of powered sugar or flour. Now stuff it down your pants. Now try to walk. Waddle much? Think walking down an airport runway like you've got an extremely full adult diaper *wouldn't* be noticed?

So what happened to Brad? Well, he was caught, of course. Once he landed in Melbourne, the customs folks frisked him and found his kilo of cocaine contraband. If he was hoping the Aussie customs folks wouldn't pat him down *down under,* he was sadly mistaken.

Source: *Herald Sun* (Australia)

EVERYBODY MUST
GET PARANOID?

One of the more unpleasant side effects of heavy pot smoking, beside the weight gain from all those munchies, is a little thing called paranoia. Paranoia is no fun; thinking people are out to get you all the time dulls your ability to determine when people actually *are* out to get you.

With this in mind, lets us suggest that "Herb" seems to us to fit the model of a long-time toker, because his paranoia seemed to be fairly advanced—advanced enough for him to believe one night that he was being robbed. It was also advanced enough for him to call 911 and communicate this belief to the operator, who duly dispatched Bozeman, Montana, police to Herb's pad. Herb directed the police to his closet, where he claimed the robber had stuffed himself in an attempt to escape detection.

The police went to the closet. They didn't find any robber, which was good news for Herb. On the other hand, they couldn't help but notice the two marijuana plants in the closet. That was *not* good news for our friend Herb, because that meant Herb was then quickly arrested for felony manufacturing of dangerous drugs. How could Herb forget about the closet stash? Well, another side-effect of prolonged pot use: short-term memory loss.

So remember, just because you're paranoid doesn't mean they're not out to get you. Especially when you *help* them.

Source: *Daily Chronicle* (Bozeman, MT)

CRACK IS WACK

We could go into long and boring detail to provide you with all the reasons why you should never do crack cocaine. But let's just cut to the chase—not only is crack an illegal substance, it also can render a person quite dumb.

Which brings us to "Betsy," of Ashland, Ohio. Betsy apparently had a hankerin' for some crack, so she picked up a friend's cell phone and made a call. To whom was she making the call? Well, she wasn't quite sure—later tapes of the call (that's a hint) have her asking the people near her, "What number was I just calling?" Well, we don't know who she intended to call, but who she *did* call should have been obvious to her when the person on the other end of the line picked up the phone and said, by way of greeting, "Ontario Police."

And yet, Betsy missed that. You ask, well, how can you miss someone actually *saying* "police?" Let's go back to our original thesis that *crack makes people stupid.* So not only did Betsy completely miss her phone partner's self-identification as a member of the law enforcement community, Betsy went on to have a chatty little conversation with the fellow before asking him, "Do you have 80?" meaning $80 worth of crack rocks. Our law enforcement professional, rather more on the conversational ball than Betsy, allowed that he might have. Betsy then asked if the stuff was good.

Our officer allows that the stuff he has is indeed good (you think he's going to say, "Nah, it's pretty bad"?), so Betsy arranges a pickup. She's so eager to settle the deal that when she's disconnected, she calls back, exhibiting the sort of focus one doesn't usually attribute to the strung out. The police get her to admit she wants to buy crack and then they arrange to meet in the parking lot of a fast food joint.

There, the policemen found her and her friends and took them into custody. Betsy, "thinking" fast, proclaimed that she was just there for some food, but the $80 in her pocket—the agreed-upon amount for the deal—suggested otherwise. Betsy's response to the discovery of the exact sum of the drug deal in her pocket: well, that's not *my* money. Did we mention that *crack makes people stupid?*

The final tally on Betsy's charges: felony soliciting (for asking the cops for crack), attempting to commit an offense, and disorderly conduct. All that could get you a year in the can. "It's the worst case of a misdialed phone number I've ever seen," said one member of the Ontario police force. And one of the easiest drug busts they'll ever have.

Source: ChannelCincinnati.com, NorthCentralOhio.com,
Port Clinton News Journal (OH)

A CASE OF BAD CRACK

Meet "Hugo," of Chalmette, Louisiana. Hugo had a taste for the crack and had settled on a barter system to acquire some from his local dealers. He traded his microwave oven for a rock. But when he got home, he discovered that he'd been totally ripped off. There was a small rock of *something* in his crack pipe, but it wasn't made out of cocaine.

What to do? As you know, cocaine is illegal so it's not as if there's a customer service hotline one can call to complain about quality. Not only that, but now Hugo was down one microwave oven. So Hugo had a "brilliant" idea; he could call 911 and complain to the cops that someone had sold him bad crack.

And so Hugo invited the cops into his place, explained the situation, and asked them if they'd like to see the rock in question. Well, of *course* the cops wanted to see it. So Hugo offered it up for their observation, still lovingly cradled in the crack pipe. This is when the police arrested him for possession of drug paraphernalia. Maj. Marcel David, chief of the St. Bernard Parish Sheriff's special investigations division, noted that it was "the first I've heard of" a drug user allowing a cop to look at his drug paraphernalia.

The rock turned out, indeed, to be totally coke free. And that's good news for Hugo. Possession of drug paraphernalia is a misdemeanor. Drug possession is a lot more serious. Of course, what *really* stinks is that Hugo still doesn't have his microwave back.

Source: *New Orleans Times-Picayune*

SHE FLIPPED THE BIRD,
HE FLIPPED THE CUFFS

We encourage all people to be nice and courteous on the road. For one thing, it's just the polite thing to do; sure, the jackass who thoughtlessly cuts you off in traffic should probably be brained with a wrench and his carcass left to fatten the crows, but you're a better person than that. For another thing, not every car on the road has a driver who will take rudeness sitting down.

"Brenda" from Arizona would have been well-advised to keep her cool on the road, for several reasons. One, she was driving with a suspended license. Two, there was marijuana in her car. Three, there was also some methamphetamine and various drug paraphernalia. All which well-nigh screamed, "Do Not Draw Attention to this Car."

But Brenda couldn't help it. As she tooled down Arizona's Highway 70 with some friends, a car behind her attempted to pass her. Brenda was having none of it and blocked the passing attempts as they occurred. Eventually the car managed to get ahead of her, and as it passed, Brenda felt motivated to honk her horn at the car and flip the other car's driver the bird. Her satisfaction at flipping off another driver was short-lived, however, because after Brenda turned into the parking lot of a nearby convenience store, the other driver pulled up and revealed himself as a cop, who had been driving an unmarked car. Surprise!

Brenda was arrested on charges of possession of marijuana, possession of marijuana for sale, transportation of marijuana for sale, possession of a dangerous drug, and pos-session of drug paraphernalia. Noted the arresting officer, "It's hilarious. I was trying to go home. They totally brought it on themselves. I wasn't even looking for them."

So please, be nice on the road. Even if you *don't* have a car full of illegal drugs.

Source: *The Eastern Arizona Courier*

THE MAP TO IDIOTVILLE

Have we mentioned yet that smoking a lot of marijuana can lead to memory loss? No? Well, if you do smoke marijuana, how can you be *sure*? See, that's our point. When you have gaps in your memory thanks to habitual toking, it can lead to all sorts of trouble.

"Dirk" and "Burke" were two "agricultural entrepreneurs," shall we say, who one day were driving near the Kentucky-Tennessee border when they noticed they were being followed by the cops. This was bad news, since the two men had some joints in their possession at the time. The duo tried tossing the pot out of the car, but strangely, the cops directly behind them seemed to catch on to that little ploy.

After pulling the two over, the police noticed maps in the car. On the maps were several locations on both sides of the state line, marked with large "X"s. And X marked what spot? Well, the spots where marijuana plants were growing in unsuspecting farmers' fields—120 plants in just one location. The total street value of the haul was estimated at about $50,000. See, if these guys hadn't had big gaps in their memories, they wouldn't have needed the maps. Sure, everyone uses maps, but if ever there was a time when one would wish to commit a location to memory, this would have been it.

Dirk and Burke were charged with manufacturing and possessing marijuana with intent to resell and tampering with evidence—the last of these charges related to tossing the joints. So do try to remember to just say no.

Source: *The Jackson Sun* (TN), CBS News

WHEN YOU'RE SNIFFING THIS STUFF, IT'S TIME FOR REHAB

Working on the principle of "When You're a Hammer, Everything Looks Like a Nail," the drug-loving burglars who were helping themselves to the contents of a Melbourne, Australia, home were thrilled when they found a wooden box with a powdery substance inside. It was powder! In a box! Just right for snorting! And so they did. It wasn't until afterward—and when, we suspect, none of them felt the usual narcotic effects of actual narcotics—that one of them began to suspect that maybe that powder in a box wasn't full of drugs after all.

Here you have to imagine these burglars wracking their drug-blunted little brains as to what else those ashes in a box could be, and then slowly, as if controlled by a rheostat turned by a tortoise, the light coming on. They weren't sniffing someone's drugs—they were sniffing *someone*.

In truth, it wasn't the cremated remains of a human. But what it actually was isn't any better. The burglars had taken a snootful of the cremated remains of the family's beloved pet goat. Leaving aside the ancillary issue of goat cremains, the fact is, no one wants to snort a goat if they can help it.

The robbers, incidentally, were eventually picked and charged with burglary and theft, and at least one of them—the one who figured out they weren't snorting drugs—pled guilty and as of this writing was still awaiting sentencing. No matter what happens, it can't be worse than inhaling an animal.

Source: *Sydney Morning Herald*

DAD, THAT'S MY COKE!

Yes, some people have issues with their fathers, but people's run of the mill daddy issues are nothing compared to the problems of South London, England, resident Shane Williams and his dad, Martin. Because although your dad might have yelled at you to turn down that damn music, or told you that he wouldn't buy you that bicycle when you were six, it's nowhere near as bad as what Martin arranged for his son.

Know, to begin, that Shane was a drug dealer, and by drug dealer, we don't mean a guy who grows a little weed in his closet. We mean like Tony "Scarface" Montana kind of drug dealer; at one point in May 2003, he had about 76 kilos of cocaine loitering in his house, a whole lot more than anyone is going to keep around for personal use. Yeah, Shane was a dealer, big time.

Martin knew about Shane's career choice, and he was concerned. Concerned that his son was a drug dealer? Well, no: he was more concerned that his son would sell all those drugs before he could steal them from him. Seems that Martin did the math on the street value of 76 kilos of blow and suddenly the wages he was pulling down as a working stiff seemed a little weak. So he told a trio of shady underworld types about his son's inventory, presumably to strike a deal. They would rob Shane, and then split the proceeds. The plan was kind of like stealing from your kid's piggy bank, if your kid was a narco kingpin.

The first part of the plan went smoothly: Martin's trio of shady friends surprised Shane and a friend and robbed them, but not before the trio took the time to taser poor Shane into submission and club his pal over the head with a crowbar. The second part, about the profit split . . . well, let's just say there was a complication. As in, the authorities were already casing Shane's place and, seeing the altercation, swooped in to arrest everyone, including Shane and Martin.

If you think this little father-son adventure caused some family tension, you'd be right. At Martin's sentencing—twenty years for robbery, conspiracy, and drug charges—Shane leaned over to dad (he was in the same docket) and reportedly encouraged him to "rot in hell." Prison is probably close enough. Of course, Shane shouldn't be feeling too smug, since he was also sentenced to twenty years for conspiracy to sell cocaine. If the British penal system had any sense of humor at all, it'd make 'em cell mates.

See, after that tale, most people's problems with their dads are nothing. So give your ol' pop a hug! But, to be on the safe side, don't tell him about any valuables you have in the house.

Source: Reuters, *Evening Standard* (UK), Scotsman.com

ANOTHER MEANING
FOR GETTING HIGH

Matt" had a certain popular—if illegal—agricultural **enthusiasm:** the Alpaugh, California, man liked growing himself a little bit of the marijuana, the illegality of which could present a problem. But Matt seemed to have it all figured out. His backyard was surrounded by a six-foot-high fence that he figured was more than tall enough to shield his gardening predilections from whatever various law enforcement officers or others might be happening to pass by.

And it would have worked, too, if Matt's thumb had not been so very green. We don't know what Matt was feeding his pot plants, but whatever it was, it turned them into prize specimens of *Cannabis Sativa,* with some of the stalks exceeding over seven feet in height! That's the marijuana equivalent of growing a hundred-pound pumpkin.

However, seven feet, if you'll recall, is taller than six feet. By about a foot, or so we're told by the measuring experts. Anyway, more than tall enough to be seen *over* the fence by the neighbors, one of whom, unimpressed with Matt's agricultural acumen, ratted out our gardening enthusiast to the cops. "Some were taller than the fence in the back yard," Tulare County Sheriff's Lt. Marsh Carter said. "It was kind of blatant. Unbelievable."

And thus did the police enter Matt's backyard with a search warrant, to find more than 50 pot plants thriving in his tender care, a collection that Tulare County Sheriff's officials estimated had a street value of more than half a million dollars. Matt redeemed all that possession for a free trip in a police car, the lucky sap, and a bail set at $75,000.

At least where Matt's likely to end up, the fences will be plenty high.

Source: *The Visalia Times-Delta* (CA)

Dim Bulbs in Bright Lights

DUDE, WHERE'S MY CAR? (2000)

Our Dumb Guys: Jesse Richmond (Ashton Kutcher) and Chester Greenburg (Seann William Scott)

Our Story: After a night of apparently intense partying, Jesse and Chester wake up with no memory of the previous night and no idea where Jesse's car could be. The two attempt to track down the car, make up with their girlfriends, and recover their memories, which leads to an adventure featuring bizarre bubble-wrapped UFO cults, transvestite strippers, tattoos, skee-ball, and—of course!—the fate of the known universe.

Dumb or Stoned? While it's clear these two are complete failures of the "Just Say No" generation (their personal nicknames are "Johnny Potsmoker" and "Smokey McPot"), and indeed believe their substance abuse is the proximate cause of their memory lapse and missing automobile, they go through the actual film in a largely chemically unaltered state. So: we have to go with dumb here.

High Point of Low Comedy: Jesse and Chester are held captive by a freakish French ostrich fancier (Brent Spiner, who played Data in *Star Trek: The Next Generation*) and must answer questions relating to those large birds or be trapped in a cage with the allegedly humorous Andy Dick.

And Now, In Their Own Words: Jesse ponders, "Is it possible that we got so wasted last night that we bought a lifetime supply of pudding and then totally forgot about it? As he opens the refrigerator to reveal said lifetime supply of pudding, Chester says, "I'd say it's entirely possible."

They're Dumb, But Is the Film Good? It depends on what your definition of "good" is. If two hours of largely thought-free, stoner-humor entertainment sounds like fun, then this is the movie for you. If those types of movies make you want to demand those two hours of your life back, then perhaps another flick may be in order.

CHAPTER 14

SEX AND OTHER NAKED ACTIVITIES

Sex and nakidity: without them, none of us would be here today. Think about it (but not *too* much, because that's a page in the tome known as "Things I Don't Wanna Think About My Parents Doing"). Sex is one of the most natural processes a human can engage in. But just because it's natural doesn't mean people don't approach it, well, unnaturally. You want proof? Then, this is the chapter for you. Enjoy.

WHEN LUST GOES OVERBOARD

We don't know much, but we know this: most people are, shall we say, *curious* about nudity. Sure, some people *say* they're not much for it, but the following story shows just how dumb the naked body can render a crowd of people.

We should also admit that there's a time and place for enjoying nudity and there are other times that are somewhat less than perfect. One of those times, it turns out, is while one is on a boat on Lake Travis, near Austin, Texas. One such boat, with about sixty people on it, was cruising along the lake when it approached a park known as Hippie Hollow. According to the official Web site, Hippie Hollow Park is famous for its rocky shoreline and "Spectacular views of Lake Travis." But as it's also the home to Texas's only clothing-optional public beach, it's also known for its spectacular views of *other* things, too.

As was apparently well-known by the folks on the boat, since as it came closer to Hippie Hollow, everyone on the boat went to the shore-facing side to get a look at the exposed bits and pieces on the beach. In their rush for ogletainment, our boat riders neglected to consider what happens to a boat with all the weight on one side.

And what does happen? Well, the boat capsizes, that's what. And suddenly sixty people hoping to get a look at nekkid folks found themselves getting something of a cold dunking (probably just what they needed). Two people were slightly injured, but most of the passengers were simply all wet. We bet the nudists on the beach enjoyed the show they got more than the people on the boat enjoyed theirs.

Source: Associated Press

THAT GREASY FREAK

We **all have our little obsessions.** Some are harmless. Some are a little strange. And then somewhere *way* past that is "Robert" and his strange preoccupation with Vaseline.

Yes, Vaseline, the world's best-loved petroleum jelly. Who knew that a product that can soothe your chapped lips can also remove eye makeup without clogging your pores? Truly, it's a miracle product with lots of good, clean uses.

Just not quite as many as Robert had for the product. Robert had been staying at a Motel 6 near Binghamton, New York; when he checked out, housekeeping went in and found that Robert had liberally applied Vaseline to everything in the room. By everything, we mean *everything:* the TV, the chairs, tables, towels, sheets, even the carpeting. After police were called to the scene, they found a trash can filled with fourteen empty Vaseline containers. In all, damage to the room cost over $1,000.

Where to find the greasy miscreant? Binghamton police had a hunch that someone who might slather one motel room might do something similar elsewhere. And wouldn't you know, they were right. Robert was apprehended at a nearby hotel, covered from stem to stern in Vaseline. And aren't you glad you're not the cop who had to handcuff *him* (think they wiped him down first so he wouldn't squirm out of the handcuffs?). But handcuff him they did, and sent him to jail, too, for "criminal mischief." There's a euphemism for you.

Source: Associated Press, *Newsday*

FROM THE "PROBABLY TOO DUMB TO BE TRUE" FILE

We just about drooled over ourselves when we saw this one while we were doing research for the book because it was just so perfect. And then we realized that it was maybe *too* perfect. Our research found the story in several different places, but each of the stories had the same source. And Snopes.com, the great Internet repository of urban legends, lists this story as "questionable." So we reluctantly have to place this one in the "of doubtful truthfulness" file. You take your chances. But it's just too good not to share.

The story involves a German couple. They've been married for eight years, and while they're otherwise happy, they've had no luck on the child front. So they go to the University Clinic of Lubek to see what might be the problem. The doctors there do a number of tests on the man and wife and discover the two of them are normally fertile; there's no biological impediment to having kids. Now, if the couple aren't having a whole lot of sex, that could complicate matters—it cuts down on the number of chances for conception. So the doctors ask the couple, "How often are you having sex?" To which the couple replies, "Having what?"

"We are not talking retarded people here," the clinic spokesperson is supposed to have said, "but a couple who were brought up in a religious environment who were simply unaware, after eight years of marriage, of the physical requirements necessary to procreate."

Now you can see why we adore this story down to its bones, and yet are *deeply* suspicious about it. The idea that two people could go through decades of life and eight years of marriage and not know about the whole sex thing. It's boggling. At last report the couple were being sex therapy lessons; *they're* in for a shock.

True or not? You make the call.

Source: Ananova

OLD SCHOOL NUDiTY

A note to nudists, if you are of advancing years, you'll want to stay well clear of the Eforie Nord resort in Romania. The police are trying to pass a law there that will make it illegal for women over the age of sixty to go topless. Apparently, law enforcement in this Black Sea hot spot has gotten complaints about older women shucking their tops and letting it all hang out.

The official line here is that all those nekkid older women might scare away the tourists, but a quote from one Romanian policeman is rather more instructive: "It's always a pleasure to see a young woman, who also has to be beautiful of course, topless on the beach," he said. "But the irony is that there are more old women going topless. I find it sometimes quite repulsive. I can understand the idea of wanting to get a uniform tan, but old women should simply give up on it."

No word from the Romanian policemen if there would be a commensurate ban, on, say, pasty old guys prancing around in Speedos, or (shiver, shiver) without them. Also, of course, no word on how many of those allegedly tourist-scaring old women are actually tourists themselves, and therefore unlikely to be frightened by their own nudity. Or, for that matter, how many of the topless old women find the police repulsive. In the meantime, our advice to the policemen is simply this: You don't *have* to look, pal.

Source: ThisisLondon.com, Ananova

A HARDCORE BENEFIT

In these times, job benefits mean more to employees than ever—and if you're a business owner, the key to attracting and retaining good workers is to offer them benefits that are relevant to their lives; benefits that will keep on giving.

Like, say, porn.

Hey, *we're* not offering it, but the Danish IT company LL Media is. It pays for its workers' subscriptions for Internet smut, so long as they view it at home and not at work. Its owners came to the decision to offer porn as a benefit to workers in a simple, matter-of-fact way. "We know that 80 percent of all hits on the Internet are on porn sites," said company director Levi Nielsen. "And we can see that people also surf porn pages during work." And remember—when it comes to benefits, you want to give the people what they want. And Nielsen stated he believed this benefit would make his staff more relaxed. Well, for starters.

This benefit might make one hesitant to get near any of the company's computer equipment. But there's a catch: as noted above, the free porn is only for home use—the company blocks all smutty sites during the work day. Work, it seems, is still meant to be work.

We doubt this will catch on over here. For one thing, who wants to be the first to ask for it? No, no. After *you*.

Source: Aftenposten

LiKE ROMEO AND JULiET, WiTH DUCTWORK

Mandy" loved **"Teddy."** Teddy loved Mandy. Oh sure, they met in an interesting way: Mandy was in Daviess County Detention Center in Kentucky for first-degree possession of a controlled substance, while Teddy was in the same facility sweating out multiple DUIs. But even their reasons for incarceration implied they had so much in common. What is love but the controlled substance of the heart?

There were, of course, complications, namely that in the United States, at least, detention facilities are not designed to allow for easy romantic moments. But where there's a will, there's a way, especially when there are also crawl spaces in the detention facility. Teddy apparently discovered that all the cells in the facility were connected by plumbing ductwork, and if one is ambitious (and we suspect, thin) enough, one can crawl through the ductwork to get to other cells for a romantic interlude.

Interestingly enough, another thing detention facilities in the United States don't offer much of is birth control, which is why Mandy found herself pregnant. Mandy and Teddy both denied any sexual contact, but you know, a baby isn't someone one can brew up one's self.

The two of them were charged with administrative violations of attempted escape, lying to a jail deputy, and interfering with the safety and security of a facility. Mandy was carted off to a separate women's facility, one that presumably does not have easily invasive piping. It seems that the course of true love still runs bumpy.

Source: *Messenger-Inquirer* (Owensboro, KY)

A LiTTLE BiT OF ROAD RAGE

Yes, it's true. Road rage makes people do strange, inexplicable things. That's why it's not called "Road Tiffs" or "Road Squabbles" or something innocuous like that. No, when you're in a road rage, you've pretty much taken leave of your senses—and in at least one case, one man took leave of his pants.

We're on the road in Laforurche Parish, Louisiana, traveling south on Highway 3235, and two cars have our attention. One is a car being driven by a woman; the other is a pick-up truck being driven by a man. The truck is hauling a trailer and going slow enough that the woman decides to pass the truck. Well, this doesn't sit very well with the driver of the truck, who honks his horn at her, and passes her and slows down intentionally to make her pass him again. As she does so, he rolls down his window, lifts up his torso, and flashes something one does not normally see poking out a car window. Yeah, that'll show her.

Alas, technology was not on the flasher's side: the woman flipped out her cell phone and called her husband, who took the license plate number and called the sheriff's office, who ran the plate and then paid a visit to the flasher in question. He admitted to driving on that road, but denied the flashing. They arrested him on obscenity charges anyway; interestingly enough, he'd been arrested on obscenity before. Some people. He was lucky the woman didn't have a camera on that cell phone.

Road Rage: best to keep it in check. Or at least keep it clothed.

Source: TheNewOrleansChannel.com

The Really Stupid Quiz

SEX AND OTHER NAKED ACTIVITIES

One of these stories is true. Two of these stories are false. Which is which? Well, that's why we call it a quiz.

1. The Italian town of Vinci—hometown of Leonardo da Vinci—has pioneered a new frontier in car-bound sex: official parking spaces. The city has set aside more than 170 parking spaces at a sports stadium where amorous couples can park their cars in the evening and go at it without fear of being arrested for indecent behavior (although presumably not on game nights). Car sex is common in Italy, where many men and women live with their parents well into their 30s, which naturally makes sexual congress at home unfeasible (or at least uncomfortable) for many. Vinci mayor Giancarlo Faenzi estimates that 90 percent of his constituency has had car sex at least once.

2. Customers at a brothel in Hamburg, Germany, were exposed to an interesting version of coitus interruptus when the workers at the brothel forced a work stoppage—not to protest working conditions but to watch the latest episode of the German version of *Big Brother*. The recent edition of *Big Brother* had been one of the steamiest yet, particularly with the antics of housemates Nadja and Lucie, who in one memorable episode did a naughty strip tease for a male housemate. "I heard one of the girls tell the others the

show was on, and then the girl I was with just stopped everything to go watch," complained one customer. Brothel managers apologized to their clients and offered "make-up" sessions, presumably when *Big Brother* was not airing.

3. A man from the former Soviet republic of Georgia had his marriage voided when it was discovered that his wife of sixteen months was a "Realdoll"—a life-size sex toy that comes in both male and female versions—and not an actual human being. Georgian officials became aware of the unusual married couple when the man began to introduce his "wife" to neighbors and produced the marriage documents when skeptical neighbors questioned him. "The husband is a very elderly man and we assume that someone felt sorry for him and allowed him to get 'married,'" said Georgian official Mikhail Kokoity. "Nevertheless we were compelled to void the marriage because it would set an unfortunate precedent." Kokoity noted that while the 'husband' could have been charged with fraudulently obtaining a marriage license, Georgian officials declined to pursue the matter further.

Answers on page 329.

The Annals of Ill-Advised Television

TODAY'S EPISODE: COUPLING

Starring in this Episode: Jay Harrington and Rena Sofer

Debut Episode: September 23, 2003, on NBC

The Pitch: Six young and good-looking friends in the big city get entangled in each other's affairs—yes, it sounds like *Friends,* but in this case, there's also a heaping helping of sex, sex, sex, and more sex. Something apparently *Friends* didn't have near enough of, despite all the kids being popped out on that show. Based on a very successful BBC comedy of the same name (which, it must be said, however, was quite obviously based on *Friends*).

It Seemed Like a Good Idea at the Time Because: *Friends* was in its last season and NBC frantically needed to find something to replace it—and what better to replace a comedy about six young friends in the big city than another comedy about six young friends in the big city?

In Reality: Trouble from the start. NBC executives were flummoxed by the first pilot generated by the U.S. show's original producers and crop of stars, so they canned the lot of them (with the exception of writer/executive producer Stephen Moffat, who was the writer of the BBC series). Critics didn't like the second go-round and were particularly harsh on the series' occupation with things carnal. After *Coupling* was canceled NBC entertainment chief Jeff Zucker cited it as a prime example of why NBC's 2003 schedule was in the dumps, saying to television critics that "some of the programming just sucked." Hey, *you* chose it, Jeff.

How Long Did It Last? Four episodes; the last episode aired on October 23rd. 10 episodes were produced, six never saw the light of day.

Were Those Responsible Punished? Too early to tell. Writer/executive producer Moffat, however, is now working on BBC's new *Dr. Who* series. Wonder if *that* will ever be remade over here.

CHAPTER 15

STUPIDITY IS MY BUSINESS, AND BUSINESS IS GOOD

The Peter Principle dictates that in business, people will rise to their level of incompetence. Our corollary to this principle is simply this: often, people don't have to rise very high to reach it. Heck, sometimes, they don't even need to get themselves into a sitting position. Lawyers, doctors, people who just have really intense attachments to their office supplies—every day, in every way, there's someone lowering the dumbness bar in the workplace.

SOME THINGS YOU
JUST CAN'T GIVE AWAY

This is not your traditional story of stupidity, to be sure, but it does say *something* about the psychology of contemporary man: a branch of Barclay's Bank in Croydon, south London, apparently wanted to gauge how much attention passers-by were paying to the advertisements in its windows. So in January 2004, the bank put up a sign in the window, inviting people to come on in and receive £5 (about $9) just for popping through the door.

Now, at this point, you may be expecting to read how the bank branch was mobbed by Britons and then perhaps how riots ensued when the bank eventually ran out.

But actually, nothing of the sort happened. In fact, nothing of *any* sort happened. And that's because in two hours that the bank had the sign in the shop, the exact number of people who popped through the door saying "Hello! I'd like my money, please!" was precisely zero. The bank literally could not give away free money. The bank chalked it up to a combination of people not reading the advertisements in the bank window, and, alternately, simply not believing that a bank would actually give money away. Expectations are more important in some cases than reality.

Incidentally, all you Londoners now planning to cruise the Croydon Barclays for your free cash can forget it. The bank spokeswoman stressed this was a one-time experiment. You missed your free money! Now don't you feel silly.

Source: BBC

TRIMMING JUSTICE

Some lawyers are known for their sartorial acumen and well-nigh metrosexual attention to matters of grooming, because nothing says "trust me" to a jury like a $4,000 suit and fingernails buffed to a fare-thee-well. But we think we're not alone in the belief that while it's perfectly acceptable if a lawyer wants to blow your $300-an-hour fee on fine Italian tailoring and pedicures, it's probably best if he or she takes care of that business outside of the courtroom.

Someone needed to tell that to "Jorma," a Finnish prosecutor working on a financial crime trial. While everyone else in the courtroom was busy working under the impression that they were, you know, in *a court of law,* he looked down at his nails and decided that what he really needed to do right that moment was give them a nice trim. And so he clipped his nails back to what he thought was an appropriate length in a rather inappropriate venue.

It's easy to see why such an action would not be appreciated. Aside from violating the polite fiction that the officers of the court are actually paying attention to the proceedings at least some of the time, we'd be betting the sharp metallic *ping* that emanates from each nail clipping can get really annoying when someone else is trying to lay down evidence. Plus it would be a real shame to catch some nail clipping shrapnel during opening statements.

How did he follow up clipping his nails? By looking at the back of his hands, deciding they were just *too* hairy, and beginning to trim those back, too. And here we go from being merely hygienically zealous to being entirely and totally gross.

Eventually the court has enough and reprimanded the prosecutor (who, it was rumored, had done trimmings in other cases as well). For a punishment, we'd suggest forcing the fellow to bite his own nails. The horror. The horror.

Source: Aftenposten

A BAD TIME TO BE OUT OF GAS

There are some sentences you just don't want to hear from your emergency medical technician while you're traveling to a hospital in an ambulance. From the obvious ("Oh, that's gotta hurt!") to the oblivious ("Wow, I always thought the spleen was on the other side of the body"), there are plenty of comments an ambulance passenger would be better off *not* hearing. But just what would happen if a traumatized ambulance patient heard the following request: "Uh, can we, like, borrow some money for gas?"

That sentence, or one close to it, came out of the lips of the EMT transporting Julia Paul, who had gone into premature labor, and her partner Chris Boag. The two were being taken from a hospital in Essex, UK, to a facility that could accommodate the premature delivery. It was a long trip—130 miles or so. Along the way the ambulance ran low on gas and stopped to refuel. In an embarrassing moment to say the least, the ambulance driver's company credit card was refused by the gas station. So the driver did the only thing he could—ask Boag if he could cough up some cash. Boag scraped up £40 (a bit over $60) before they could all be on their way.

Interestingly, the fuel-starved ambulance was actually the *second* ambulance called to transport the mom-to-be and her partner; the first developed a flat tire. It's no wonder that the British government eventually investigated this ambulance company for its attempt to pass on its transportation costs directly to the patient.

What does this tell us? One, don't go into premature labor in Essex. Two, if you *do,* make sure you've got some spare cash on you. Just in case. By the way—the baby (a girl!) and the mother were doing just fine after the birth. So at least *that* worked out well.

Source: *The Sun* (UK), *The Guardian* (UK)

NO WATER FOR ME?
THEN NO TIP FOR YOU

Parched? Thirsty? Choking on a cracker and need something to wash it down? You'll want to avoid Atlantic Hotel in Newquay, Cornwall, in the United Kingdom. For if you go there, they will refuse to serve water from the tap. It's either expensive bottled water for you—or you can drink nothing.

So learned one customer of the Atlantic Hotel's restaurant in February 2004. Mrs. Sally Burchell had gone to luncheon there for £18.50 a pop (about $30 U.S.) with about fifty other people. During the course of the meal she felt the need for simple hydration and asked a member of the staff for some tap water, which in most parts of the civilized world comes for free. She was refused and was told she could either shell out 80 pence (about $1.25) for a small bottle of water or £2 ($3.20) for a liter of the stuff. Mrs. Burchell thought this was mildly outrageous and wrote a complaint letter about it to the hotel manager.

The hotel manager, by the name of Anthony Cobley, wrote back, not to express his condolences to a disgruntled customer but to "enlighten you about the workings of the modern world." He detailed that in the modern world, there's no such thing as a free glass of water. Let's let his words do the talking, shall we?

> "I buy water from the South West Water company. I buy the glasses that the water is served in. I buy the ice that goes into the water and I buy the labour to serve the water.

"I provide the luxury surroundings for the water to be drunk in and again pay for the labour and washing materials to wash the glass after you have used it, and you think that I should provide all of this free of charge!

"As regards your comment that you will not be returning to the Atlantic Hotel ever again, leaves me to say that customers who only drink water and complain about paying for it, I can certainly do without."

That's customer service?

Incidentally, according to the BBC, "The actual cost of a litre of tap water is less than a ten thousandth of a penny according to South West Water." So charging £2 for a liter is something like a 20,000 percent markup. Which even for a place proving "luxury surroundings" does seem to be a little steep.

Cobley may have saved some infinitesimal fraction of a pence in not providing his customer with a glass of water, but his letter of unrepentant tightwaddedness showed up in media outlets all over the world, from the BBC to, well, this very book. One can imagine the negative impact on Cobley's business. So in the interest of enlightening future hotel managers of the world to the workings of the modern world: when someone asks for some water, get it for them, already. And *smile.*

Source: Ananova, BBC

"NOBODY ASKED"

Now, admittedly, these days so many former high-ranking business executives are being frog-marched into jail, it's getting harder and harder to find an exec who isn't an ex-con. To be clear, let's admit there's a difference between the guy who maybe screwed up as a youth and went to the slammer, and then cleaned up his life, and the guys who get to the executive suite and then think of new and exciting ways to obfuscate the corporate accounting, The latter are jerks; the former may be worthy of having some slack cut for them. Be that as it may, it's best that the executives and board members not have criminal records that reflect poorly on the company or its product. So one might not wish to have a former drug dealer as chairman of a pharmaceutical company, or an alcoholic minding the still.

Not that something like that could ever happen, you say? Meet James Joseph Minder, who was for a brief time in 2004 the chairman of the board for Smith & Wesson, America's second-largest gun company, famous for its handguns and its close association to law enforcement. His brief time as chairman probably had something to do with a little story the *Arizona Republic* newspaper ran about him. It turns out that Minder had spent fifteen years in prison for armed robbery, while he was a student at the University of Michigan in the 1950s.

To be fair to Minder, after he was finally sprung from prison in 1969, he led an exemplary public life and had run a nonprofit agency to help troubled and disabled Michigan teens for two decades. So once he put that armed robbery thing behind him, he turned out to have been rehabilitated just fine. Sometimes the system does work well enough for a former (and reformed) armed robber to lead a gun company.

In an era where applicants for janitorial and executive assistant positions are scrutinized with invasive background checks, how does someone with several armed robberies in his history slip by? Minder's answer is instructive: "Nobody asked." Indeed. Time for some background checks in boardrooms, we say. We imagine the janitors and assistants cheering. Quietly.

Source: Ananova, *USA Today,* CNNMoney.com

IT'S NEVER TOO EARLY TO
DEVELOP SOUL-CRUSHING DEBT

It's not the credit card application that was unusual. It was
pretty much the same as most other offers that promise pre-
approval, low-monthly interest, and all that jazz.

What was unusual was that the recipient, one Miss Abi
McDermott Knott of Leeds, England, was thirteen months old
at the time she received it. Which, even by the rather lax standards of credit card issuers today, seems a *little* premature. After
all, that's hardly enough time to build a credit history, now, is
it? What has she really bought with her own money? Not a whit.

Babies—cute though they are and necessary for the sur-
vival of the species—are totally financial freeloaders. Other
people spring for their food, their shelter, and the clothes. No
matter how you look at them, babies are just a bad credit risk.
Have one if you want—have two, they're small—but banks'
issuing them credit cards is just not good policy.

Which Ian Barber, the appropriately apologetic
spokesman for Barclaycard, the credit card issuer in question,
readily admitted, "There's absolutely no way that she would
have been issued with a card," he said. Of course, that's easy to
say after the baby turned down the offer. Or so mother Shelley
Roberts claims: "I asked her if she wanted to apply but she
didn't seem too interested, oddly enough."

Source: BBC, *Sydney Morning Herald*

AN IMPORTANT TIP
FOR FUNERAL DIRECTORS

Funeral directors are busy, what with people dying all the time. Still, we thought we'd pass along a small piece of advice (that really should go without saying). Before sending a coffin off to be buried in the cemetery, do the nice thing and make sure it's the right one. A case of mistaken identity is no picnic for an undertaker. And of course, it's difficult for the family of the deceased as well.

Such was the problem during the funeral of Mary Fitzsimmons of Wallyford, Scotland. At the graveside, over a hundred family and friends had gathered to say their final goodbyes, and Mary's pallbearers—her adult children—were lowering the coffin into the family plot. As the it was lowered into the grave, grieving son Kevin took a final look at the coffin . . . and noticed the name "Wilson" on the plaque on the outside.

Thus the funeral came to a screeching halt as the embarrassed funeral directors took away the casket of the mysterious Wilson and went looking for poor Mary Fitzsimmons. The mourners were left cooling their heels for an hour until the undertakers returned. As Kevin told the press, "Burying your mother is difficult enough without this kind of thing."

Fortunately for the undertakers, the family accepted their apologies and said they had no plans to seek compensation for the screw-up. So, mortuary professionals, remember: check those coffins. Because this isn't merely the kind of mistake that lasts a lifetime, it lasts an eternity.

Source: *The Daily Record* (UK), *The Scotsman*

HE MUST REALLY
LOVE HIS STAPLERS

Some people, it seems, have a really unhealthy relationship with their office supplies. Take for instance, "Edward," who worked in an office in North Platte, Nebraska. One day the supervisors of the office sent out a memo: from now on, it said (more or less), only the manager of the office would have the keys to the supply cabinets. The era of free pens and staples, it seems, was at an end in this little corner of cubicle land.

We imagine the memo was generally unpopular, on the grounds that people who are adults don't like the implication that they can't be trusted. But Edward's reaction was, shall we say, more dramatic than the norm: Edward took a copy of the memo out of the office, got it up close and personal with a .22 caliber handgun, and perforated it with a lot of lead. Edward then returned the bullet-ridden memo to its position in the office. As if that wasn't enough to give Edward's coworkers the hot and cold running heebie-jeebies, consider that two days later he called the office secretary to declare he wasn't coming in to work because he felt like he might just up and shoot somebody. Several coworkers were so put-off by Edward's expression of his true feelings that they rushed out to get protection orders.

Edward's profession? Mental health practitioner and professional counselor, of course. And was his license revoked in Nebraska, on the grounds of unprofessional conduct? Oh my, *yes*. We hope for everyone's sake he was allowed to take his paper clips with him.

Source: Associated Press, *World-Herald* (Omaha, NE)

A REFRESHING MOMENT
OF HONEST, CORPORATE GREED

Americans like to think they have cornered the market on corporate greed and outperform everyone else out there. It's hard to argue—look at Enron and then tell us that when it comes to corporate greed the United States doesn't *totally* rock the house. Whoo-hoo! We *are* the champions, our friend. But it's not to say that we can't appreciate a well-turned moment of blatant corporate greed elsewhere on the globe. Just as a Yankees fan can appreciate the efforts of the Yomiuri Giants, so can an aficionado of U.S. corporate gormlessness appreciate it when it raises its greedy head in other nations on the globe.

Which is why we wish to raise a glass in toast to Telstra, Australia's largest telecommunications provider, which enjoys approximately 90 percent of the market for line rentals in Australia. In May 2004 Telstra decided that one of the things it would like to do is charge its customers a little extra if they used a credit card to pay their monthly bills. Telstra's managing director for finance and administration, John Stanhope, addressed an Australian Senate committee on the subject. When Senator Sue Mackay asked Stanhope why the company decided to impose the new charge, he brazenly replied: "Because we are able to."

Wow. Think about that for a minute. If an American company officer came to a Senate Committee to explain a totally new and dubious charge, you just know he or she would skate around the subject with some mumbo-jumbo like "increasing value to the customer" or "leveraging cost structures across multiple revenue streams" or "actualizing corporate synergies." Because here in America, we're okay with greed, just not *naked* greed. Not only is naked greed pasty and flabby and icky, it's stupid to admit to it.

But in Australia, naked greed is getting a nice all-over tan: Down Under, Telstra saw the customer, ripe for the plucking, and boy, did those customers get plucked. They got plucked hard. And really, why deny it? Why do customers exist if *not* to get royally plucked? That's their contribution to the whole circle of finance. Sure, Stanhope went on to note that Telstra pays a service charge to the card companies and that the new customer charge is meant in some way to recoup that charge. But once you've established that you're charging people more just because you can, any further rationale is just frosting on the mudpie.

What's even better, the senator then asked Stanhope, if you're charging extra to pay with a credit card, are you giving discounts to people who pay by cash? "The assumption of course is doing it by cash is less costly," Stanhope replied. "That isn't necessarily the case, it might be as costly as other methods." In other words, hold on to your feathers, Telstra customers. You're still being plucked.

Source: *The Age,* news.com.au

RABID LAWYER PUT DOWN

When you're watching a legal thriller on TV or in the movies, it's fun to watch lawyers shouting at the judges, badgering the witnesses, or otherwise doing things that make the life of a lawyer more interesting than filling up all those long billable hours. However, when your lawyer starts acting screwy in the real world it's more likely to make you reach for the Mylanta than the popcorn.

"Screwy" is an apt description of the behavior of "Daniel," a New York lawyer who was representing a middleman who brought products to the attention of manufacturers. This middleman was suing former clients, a married pair of de-signers, for breech of contract. Daniel represented his own client zealously—too zealously for the married couple, who complained during their deposition that Daniel had sent them "mad-dog lawyer's letters." When the phrase popped up again in court, Daniel barked. Like the mad-dog lawyer he was sup-posed to be. Then he claimed merely to be clearing his throat.

Bad lawyer, no barking! State Supreme Court Justice Charles Ramos slammed Daniel during a later review of the case, and noted that this behavior among other nasty tactics raised "serious concerns about fitness to practice law." He fined Daniel $8,500 for his barking, which is a lot of kibble no matter how you cut it. To make things worse, Daniel had also lost the case. All that bad behavior for nothing.

Daniel is reportedly planning to appeal the fine. If he loses the appeal, will he literally be in the doghouse?

Source: *Newsday, New York Law Journal*

MALPRACTICE
OR MONKEY BUSINESS?

We have a good feeling that if we were to look up the word "chutzpah" in the dictionary, the picture that would go along with it would be of Dr. Randall J. Smith, who until recently had a practice in Gresham, Oregon. The reason for this is two-fold, and began when a female patient came to his office for treatment of pain in her pelvis area.

Well, Dr. Smith knew how to fix that. He reportedly explained to the woman that massaging certain "trigger points" would help ease her pain. Unlike most doctors, Dr. Smith's offer to massage "trigger points" was closer to an offer to see his etchings than a diagnosis. So soon enough Dr. Smith and the patient were making the beast with two backs, so to speak.

Aside from sleeping with his patients, a treatment not taught by the leading medical schools, Dr. Smith's moxie goes one step further. Dr. Smith *billed* the Oregon Health Plan for these "treatments" to the tune of $5,000. That's submitting false health care claims, and that's a felony.

When the state of Oregon finally caught up with Dr. Smith and his innovative therapeutic techniques (and the creative billing thereof), it asked him to be its guest in one of the state's fine correctional institutions for sixty days. Also, Oregon revoked his license to practice medicine in the state. Add to that 200 hours of community service, $1,105 in fines, and probation for eighteen months as part of the plea agreement. So, ironically, you could say Dr. Smith really did pay for his sex. That's what chutzpah gets you sometimes.

Source: Reuters

YOU MUST BE THIS THIN
TO GET YOUR FISH AND CHIPS

It's not as if the average Brit was known for being svelte, but over the last twenty-five years, the number of British subjects who could be classified as "obese" has tripled to 20 percent of the men and 24 percent of the women. They're not as fat as Americans on average, but you know the Brits have gumption and a will to succeed. Americans certainly don't doubt their ability to catch up.

Neither does the British Medical Association, which in May 2004 offered up an innovative suggestion to keep chunky Brits from getting to their daily feedings of fat and salt from their local fast food chains. To quote Dr. Simon Minkoff, of the British Medical Association's junior doctors' committee: "Over-eating is not good for you—we want the government to show that it is tough on obesity by fitting narrow doorways."

In simple language: they aimed to keep overweight people from getting into fast-food joints by making the doorways too narrow for fat people to enter.

Well, just how narrow are we talking about? Try 30 centimeters (that's just under one foot for Americans). (For comparison's sake, the average American door is about 3 feet wide.) Men and women who were not clinically obese could still slide through the one-foot door, no doubt with some huffing and puffing, but those who had packed on the pounds wouldn't be able to squeeze themselves through the doorway.

Naturally, others have described this plan as cruel to plump Brits; a dietitian from the charity Weigh Concern said,

"It's discriminating and unkind. It's saying to overweight people that it's their fault," while a spokesperson for McDonald's—*not* a disinterested party, by the way—wondered how those in wheelchairs would get through such thin doors. And what if those wheelchair-bound were also clinically obese? Now, see, *there's* a quandary.

We are neutral about the idea of super-skinny doors to block super-sized fast food customers, but we've got two words to describe why such a plan wouldn't work: *Drive Through.*

Source: *The Sun* (UK)

Dim Bulbs in Bright Lights
FORREST GUMP (1994)

Our Dumb Guy: Forrest Gump (Tom Hanks)

Our Story: A slow but good-natured southern gentleman (Hanks) sits on a bench and recounts his life story to whomever passes by; as it turns out, Forrest has inadvertently played a role in nearly every single major social event between the 1950s and the 1980s, from Elvis to Apple Computers.

Dumb or Stoned? Forget about dumb—Forrest Gump is so darn *square* that it wouldn't even occur to him to *get* stoned, even on New Year's Eve in New York.

High Point of Low Comedy: After being injured in the buttocks and winning the Congressional Medal of Honor, Forrest Gump is rhetorically told by President Lyndon Johnson that Gump's posterior injury is one he'd like to see. Forrest, alas, is not nearly smart enough to know that the request is rhetorical and obliges right then and there.

And Now, In His Own Words: Forrest, on his investment in Apple Computers: "Lieutenant Dan got me invested in some kind of fruit company. So then I got a call from him, saying we don't have to worry about money no more. And I said, that's good! One less thing."

He's Dumb, But Is the Film Good? The film is so good, it gets flack from people who believe it's not as good as it is. In reality, it's a very clever film aimed at Baby Boomers, to be sure, but Hank's performance gives it a center and a gravity that makes it works marvelously. It's *very* good in every sense of the word.

CHAPTER 16

THE THRILL OF VICTORY, THE AGONY OF STUPIDITY

Like all people everywhere, we love the intense competition and rivalry of sports, but we also like the really dumb things, too. Fortunately for us, the sports world—from the kids' leagues all the way up the food chain to the pros—is positively riddled with the sort of sports jerks who fill our need for muscle-headed goofs and screw-ups. We can just sit back in our box seat, eat a $5 hot dog, and enjoy.

NOTHING TECHNICAL
ABOUT THIS KNOCKOUT

We don't believe in shooting guns at anyone—that's just rude—much less shooting guns at an athlete of international stature. But of all the athletes of international stature that shouldn't be shot at, at the top of the list, in an uncontested decision, stands Mexico's light-heavyweight champion Arturo "The Graduate" Rivera.

It seems that Rivera was stepping outside of a gym in Ciudad Juarez, Mexico, in June 2004. A gunman approached him and unloaded two pistols in Rivera's general direction. None of the bullets actually hit Rivera, an unfortunate outcome for the gunman. Perhaps this was why the gunman came out to play with two guns instead of one: he knew he had to compensate for some really bad aim.

Well, the gunman had his fun; now it was Rivera's turn. Before the shooting, Rivera's record included sixteen knockout decisions; shortly thereafter, he had seventeen. The gunman was off to the hospital where he was treated for head injuries. Also, of course, he was arrested. The police are treating it as an attempted murder—on the part of the gunman, not by Rivera.

Let's hope for everyone's sake there's no rematch.

Source: Reuters

WHEN YOU GOTTA GO, YOU GOTTA GO

You want to know what's interesting? We'll tell you what's interesting. What's *not* interesting is that right in the middle of a soccer match for the Union des Associations Européennes de Football (UEFA) Cup, Marseille goaltender Fabien Barthez felt the need to relieve himself. And what's additionally *not* interesting is that when Barthez felt his need, he proceeded to do just that, on the soccer pitch, in the middle of a game, in front of 60,000 spectators in Marseille's Velodrome stadium.

No, what's *interesting* is that no one at the game—not the other players, not the coaches, and apparently not the 60,000 spectators—noticed that Barthez watered the turf until *after* the game. There are pictures of the event, so we may presume at least one photographer had his eye on the real action. But the story didn't leak, as it were, until a caller to a French radio show passed on the rumor of Barthez's on-field micturation.

Inquiring minds want to know: how do 60,000 people miss something like that? Here in the United States, were Derek Jeter or Brett Farve suddenly to answer the call of nature on the field, it would be noticed. The answer, as a spectator at the game told *The Sun* newspaper in the U.K.: "I don't think anyone noticed at the time because we were all watching Marseille attacking at the other end."

Well, gee whiz. That explains it.

Source: *The Sun* (UK)

BEER! HOCKEY FANS! WHAT COULD POSSIBLY GO WRONG?

Our suggestions as to why the management of the Tampa Bay Lightning ice hockey team thought it was a fine idea to offer free beer to fans during the 2004 playoffs:

1. They wanted to give the crowd the slipping and sliding feeling they'd get from walking out into the ice, without actually disrupting the game.

2. Why limit the brawls to just the players?

3. Because in this era of diluted play and boring defensive strategy, you'd *have* to be drunk to enjoy NHL hockey.

The real reason was none of the above (at least, so the Lightning management *says*). The team simply wanted to try to sell some season tickets for the upcoming year. So during the first game of the Eastern Conference playoffs, the team announced on the scoreboard that anyone who put down $100 toward season tickets would get free beer during the game. To many of the folks at the game (and as it was reported immediately afterward) the implication was you could get as much beer as you wanted—an endless cup of hoppy goodness with which to wash away your cares during the game (which the Lightning won, incidentally, to what one assumes were the beerier-than-usual cheers of the home crowd).

After the entirely predictable and not-entirely-outraged responses from police and groups battling drunk driving, the Lightning management realized they had a promotion hangover on their hands and quickly backtracked. For one thing, they explained, it wasn't as if people who put down deposits on season tickets were given a personal beer bong and a monkey to tend the keg. What they got were vouchers that let them get four 12-oz beers. What's more, those vouchers could have also been redeemed for soft drinks, in case a prospective buyer's drug of choice was caffeine and not alcohol. Funny the Lightning didn't lead with the "Free Soda!" announcement.

Eventually, however, the Lightning voluntarily stuffed themselves into the penalty box, canceling the promotion and issuing an apology to those offended by the promotion. "In the end, it was a bad promotion," the Lightning's chief operating officer, Sean Henry, told the *Tampa Tribune*. "It offended a few people and it didn't drive sales." It's the last of these, we suspect, that *really* hurt: Only twenty-five people out of a crowd of than 21,425 were willing to take the Lightning up on their free beer offer. All that bad publicity for so little benefit.

Source: *Tampa Tribune*, TSN.ca

THE ROCKET'S RED WHEEZE

Hey, like any red-blooded American and/or pyromaniac, we just adore fireworks. There's nothing like the rocket's red glare to get us all Oooh-y and ahhh-y. Fireworks and sports events? Made for each other, of course! If you can't have fireworks going on with a home run or at half time, you might as well just go home.

Perhaps banking on every American's attraction to bright exploding things, the management of the football-playing Corpus Christi Hammerheads arranged to have a fireworks display before the start of their game against the San Angelo Stampede (which, we'll note, the Hammerheads defeated 29–28. Rock on, Hammerheads!). It would be a perfect start to a great game—the fireworks above the field before the game would set the scene for the athletic fireworks on the field during the game.

One small detail: the Hammerheads play football indoors.

Does this matter? It does when the firework display goes awry, as it did this night, and a blue wave of fireworks smoke starts filling the arena, as it did at the Corpus Christi Memor-ial Coliseum. To make matters worse, the arena doesn't have roof vents to let the smoke escape. What you end up with in that case is the audience pouring out of the stadium, a couple people carried away on stretchers for smoke inhalation, and all sorts of people taking oxygen hits because their asthma has been aggravated. Now that's the way to get a crowd worked up before the game! "I can't explain what happened," said

Hammerheads owner Chad Dittman. Well, Chad, three words: Fireworks. Indoors. *No.*

And happily enough, Dittman agreed: "It will be the last time we have fireworks," he told the press. Hammerheads fans—and their lungs—thank you.

Source: Associated Press, IntenseFootballLeague.com

RUMORS OF MY DEATH SOMETHING, SOMETHING, SOMETHING

It was a very sad day for the Carlisle Cricket Club in Carlisle, England, when they heard that one of their own, Leonard Brunton, had gotten himself into something of a sticky wicket; namely, he was dead. For years Brunton, or "Bunt" as he was called down the pub, had served as batsman, umpire, and groundsman for the team. Oh, very sad, it was. And so the boys did the right thing: before a game they had a moment of silence, and one of his teammates spoke of him, and they even lowered the flags at the cricket field. Someone suggested that perhaps they might send some flowers, and had one of the boys call the widow to find out where they should be delivered.

The answer: nowhere, since Bunt himself answered the phone. Either the dead had risen and were playing cricket in Carlisle, or this particular Bunt had never been laid down. And while the idea of zombie cricketers is a fine one—finally, a group utterly at peace with the pace of the game!—the whole "not dead yet" thing was probably more likely. What happened was that somebody from the cricket team had read an obit in the newspaper for someone who had the nickname of "Bunt." Reasoning that no one else could possibly have the same nickname, he went and spread the news of their old mate's passing. Good thing for Bunt his nickname wasn't "Tiny" or "Doc." He'd have had six or seven memorials by now.

Bunt received the news of his passing pretty well: He didn't keel over in shock or anything. ""It was very weird but I'm glad to say I'm very much alive," Bunt told the BBC. "Now I'm going to go and have a drink with them to prove I'm still here." One wonders, when Bunt finally does pass on, if his cricket club will actually believe it.

Source: BBC, *News & Star* (Carlisle, UK)

A PROMOTION THAT'S
JUST CRIMINAL

June 2, 2004, was two things. First, it was the tenth anniversary of the arrest of O. J. Simpson for the murder of his estranged wife Nicole and her pal Ron Goldman. Second—it was Sport Criminals Night at T. R. Hughes Ballpark in O'Fallon, Missouri, home of the minor league River City Rascals!

Yes, in this wacky promotion—a celebration of delightful intersection of sports and the criminal world—the entire stadium would be turned into a prison! Fans who wore the jersey of a pro athlete convicted of a crime would get free admission. This ruled out O.J., since he was acquitted, but never fear: A trading card with an accused athlete—which O.J. certainly was—would get you past the turnstiles. There was a trivia contest on sport criminals, prison-themed snacks (bread and water! Just $1!), and every inning, some lucky fan would be thrown into "dugout jail"—all the fun of incarceration, without an annoying shiv in the kidneys.

"We know some will be offended by this," Rascals spokesman Phil Giubileo told *St. Louis Post-Dispatch* sports columnist Bernie Miklasz. "But we're always aggressive in our promotions. Ninety-nine percent of what we do is family friendly and wholesome. But you've got to throw a curveball every now and then." Well sure. Because if you *can't* have edgy fun yukking it up with your kids over sports heroes who have murdered, raped, or assaulted other people, you're just an old stick in the mud. Dugout jail for you!

So how did Sports Criminals Night go? Well, it *didn't*, because apparently the fans of the River City Rascals thought it was a horrible, terrible idea to glorify the acts of cretinous athletes, and weren't shy about letting the team know. The promotion was canceled the day after it was announced. On the Rascals Web site, the team backtracked with the rationalization that "Our intent wasn't to honor or celebrate any criminal acts that were committed or alleged by a professional athlete, and was actually an attempt to identify how the media has changed in recent years as a result of these incidents." Yes, we can see how offering free admission to people wearing jerseys of criminals is all about the *media*.

Our suggestion for a replacement event: Promotion Director Piñata. Hey, they've already got the bats.

Source: *St. Louis Post-Dispatch,* Associated Press

The Really Stupid Quiz

THE THRILL OF VICTORY, THE AGONY OF STUPIDITY

One story is a home run of truth. Two stories are fan-clobbering foul balls of patent lies. Can you tell the difference? We'll just see about that.

1. The next time you gripe out pro athletes being overpaid babies, consider the soccer players of Mioveni, in Romania. As with many professional athletes, they believed the hard work they were doing on the field was underappreciated and undercompensated by the team owners. So, as a team, they demanded a raise in pay. And as a team, the owners canned them and immediately went looking for new players. How much more money did the players demand? Oh, about $8 a month. The team owners, who are also the city council members of Mioveni, called the pay raise demand "outrageous" and said "If they won't accept the salary on offer then they can get on with their lives while we look for replacements. It's as simple as that."

2. A "friendly" game of darts between "Pat" and "Jamie" in County Cork, Ireland, became a lot less friendly as Pat began to complain about Jamie's throwing technique. This so incensed Jamie that he raised the stakes and challenged Pat to a duel—an *actual* duel. "The pair of them went out the pub with their darts, stood back to back, counted off ten paces and then started throwing darts at each other,"

said one witness. Jamie's throwing technique prevailed, since he nailed Pat in the head with a well-aimed throw. Sadly for Jamie, even in Ireland, that's assault, and that's a trip down the gaol for him, while Pat was off to the local hospital, but at least they both emerged with their honor intact.

3. South Korean soccer fans got an astronomical site in July 2004 when a striker on the Suwon Samsung Bluewings dropped his shorts and mooned the home team fans of the Chonbuk Hyundai team at the Jeonju World Cup Stadium, after the Bluewings tipped the ball into the goal. "Our guy decided that the fans had been rude and wanted to return the favor," said Bluewings coach Cha Bum-keun told reporters. "I understand his frustration but I can't say I'm pleased with the actions." Play was stopped briefly as angry fans both pelted the field with drink cups and in several cases dropped their own pants to return the favor.

Answers on page 329.

The Annals of Ill-Advised Television
TODAY'S EPISODE: XFL

Starring in this Episode: The XFL, a new football league, featuring Jesse Ventura as an announcer

Debut Episode: February 3, 2001

The Pitch: It's football, reimagined by World Wrestling Entertainmet impresario Vince McMahon and half-owned by NBC. In this version, the sport would be rougher (no mamby-pamby kicking for the extra point after a touchdown—it's the two-point conversion or nothing!) and would feature interactive elements like microphones in huddles and cameras in cheerleader locker rooms. Games would run in the February through April interim between the end of the football season and the beginning of the baseball season.

It Seemed Like a Good Idea at the Time Because: It promised to combine the two most fanatical sports audiences—for wrestling and for football—into one huge beefy unit.

In Reality: The opening numbers for the XFL were huge; 54 million people tuned in the first week. But then the floor fell out; the vaunted "smashmouth" play was in reality just sloppy, and the ham-handed attempts to inject wrestling-style drama (including a "feud" between announcer Ventura and one of the coaches) were lame. Wrestling fans didn't get the drama they loved; football fans suspected that a football league run by people from wrestling would eventually choose scripts over sports. Five weeks after the debut, one game garnered a 1.6 rating, which was the lowest prime time rating ever registered by any program of any kind in the entire history of network television. Talk about a fumble.

How Long Did It Last: One league season, which was twelve weeks (ten regular season, two playoffs). In May 2001, Vince McMahon officially closed the league. NBC and WWE are estimated to have lost $70 million between them on their little football adventure.

Were Those Responsible Punished? As if. McMahon still runs his very successful wrestling empire, while NBC by all indications is still on the air. Jesse Ventura went back to his day job as governor of Minnesota, and one assumes that many of the XFL's football players went back to *their* day jobs, too.

CHAPTER 17

TILL DUMB
DO US PART

We like marriage; it's better than Yahtzee. Better than Triple Yahtzee, even (and it doesn't get much better than that). But even the best couples, the most harmonious matrimonial states, have their moments of abject idiocy. And the stories you are about to read—well, let's just say that most of these aren't exactly perfect marriages. Or if they were, they certainly weren't after the events shared herein.

GOIN' TO THE CHAPEL AND WE'RE GONNA STEAL THE CANDLEHOLDERS

Marriage is a blessed institution, but paying for a wedding can be damned expensive. Everything about them costs money, from the wedding dress, meant to be worn only once, to the costs of the little centerpieces at each table at the reception. But if you've got imagination, ingenuity, and a willingness to make a few opportunities where none previously existed, you can bring down the cost of your wedding quite a bit.

Just ask "Maude," an Aussie woman who was planning to wed to an American she met over the Internet. Maude wanted to make sure she didn't start her married life in a financial hole, so she decided that instead of paying for her wedding, she'd simply steal it. With that goal in mind, Maude and a willing accomplice embarked on a three-month shoplifting spree to nick what she needed for the happiest day of her life.

She did pretty well. For the reception, she stole china and cutlery as well as tumblers and wine glasses for drinks. Guests used stolen ashtrays and danced to music played on a stolen stereo, while stolen trimmings, balloons, candles, and lights added to the feloniously festive atmosphere. And what about the ceremony itself? One of the groomsmen was outfitted in a stolen suit and tie, and the bride herself—clearly far too deep in the criminal hole to be described as "blushing"—wore a purloined wedding dress worth more than $1400 (in Australian dollars). All told Maude pilfered more than $5,000 worth of wedding-related stuff.

Maude saved a bundle on the wedding, but there *was* a price to pay, as she learned when the cops showed up at the door to reclaim the pilfered items, and to arrest her for handling stolen goods, theft, and possessing the proceeds of crime. They also tacked on assaulting police, since the dainty Maude threatened to spit on the cops. So much for newlywed joy.

Maude was sentenced to two months in jail (suspended for one year), a sum of time that wasn't that much shorter than her marriage, which unraveled in just six months. Add in the three months Maude spent stealing stuff for the wedding, and she spent nearly as much time preparing and then paying for her wedding as she spent actually being married. Maybe she should have eloped.

Source: News.com.au, *The Age* (Australia)

A HOT TIME IN THE OLD CAR

Have a hankerin' to perform a sex act in a semipublic place to spice up the old marriage? It sure is risky, so here's one tip: make sure there are no warrants out for your arrest, or you might run into the unusual bit of *coitus interruptus* that afflicted a Denver area couple in May 2004.

Seems that our married couple had the desire to take their connubial bliss on the road, so they drove up to the Dillon Reservoir in the Rocky Mountains for a little bit of that good ol' fashioned backseat action. While they were enjoying the privileges of marriage, a passing deputy happened to notice there was a moon rising and stopped to investigate. Once he determined the couple were engaging in activities that were both consensual and matrimonial, our deputy ran a background check on the two and determined the husband had an outstanding warrant.

It was nothing serious—it was a dog-at-large charge (that will teach you to keep your pets on a leash)—but it was an outstanding warrant all the same, and the deputy was obliged to discharge it. So the deputy told our amorous fellow to cough up the fine: $63. Well, our man was caught a little short, as it were, and so everyone had to take a trip down to an ATM, and then to the county jail, where the fine was paid. And then our couple, we assume, went home lighter in the wallet and with their fiery passion well and truly doused. We're guessing they'll be keeping their activities homebound for a while now.

Source: *The Summit Daily News* (CO)

INAPPROPRIATE USE OF LIMOS ABOUNDS!

Boy, have we got a cautionary tale for you folks today, based on the story of "Lester" and "Lily," a couple from Boston, Massachusetts, both of whom are driving limos, which they owned.

First, let's start off with the men. Men, let's say you're married to a woman, and the two of you are estranged but trying to patch things up. If that is the case, you should not be, as one policeman put it, "enjoying the company of an unidentified female" in the back of the limo you own, especially if you've parked the limo somewhere your wife can find you. The reasons for this should be clear enough. Okay? Groovy.

Now, ladies, let's say you're driving along in *your* limo and you see your husband's limo parked somewhere, and you find said husband enjoying the company of an unidentified female. Enraged though you may be, do not hop back into your own limo and use it to ram your husband's limo. It's not nice to the limo. It's not the limo's fault your husband is a sleezebag. Okay? Groovy.

Back to the men. Men, let's say your wife is slamming her limo into your limo because of some crazy misunderstanding about an unidentified woman who may or may not have been in the back seat of your limo. Do not flee in that limo. Because if you try to flee in the limo, your wife may chase you with her limo, ramming into your limo several times during a chase where the two of you reach speeds of 50 miles an hour. Really, that's just not safe.

Once more with the ladies. Women, if you are tempted to chase after that man who is trying to escape your righteous wrath and ram his vehicle over and over and over again, well, won't you please think of the children? Specifically, the four children in the backseat of your limo, between the ages of two and thirteen? It's just a hunch we have, but we believe strongly that, aside from the issue of putting the children in extreme physical danger by ramming another car at high speeds, there's also the fact that, really, no amount of therapy is ever going to make that memory right.

Needless to say, Lester and Lily did all of these things. Lily got arrested on multiple charges, including assault with a dangerous weapon and driving to endanger. Lester is now the owner two smashed up limos. The kids were taken to the hospital for observation and then released to relatives. The unidentified female, who was in Lester's limo for the chase scene, got the hell out of these as soon as possible (and who can blame her).

In case you're wondering, Lester told reporters that the reconciliation is now off. You know, we'd guessed that already.

Source: *Boston Globe*

HE'LL BE SHOPPING
FOR A RADIATOR GRILLE

You see them all the time. Guys standing around, that blank look in their eyes, while their women do whatever shopping that needs to be done in whatever store it is they need to shop in. Most men understand that it's part of the whole "for good and bad" thing that gets slipped into the wedding vows.

"Arturo" of Miami, Florida, was having none of that junk. His wife was dawdling in a store and Arturo just had other things to do. So he stomped out of the store and got into his car. This was followed shortly thereafter by said car crashing through the front of the store. That'll get her attention, Arturo! Although, what with the police who will follow up, maybe it won't get you out of the store afterward.

Upon later questioning, Arturo denied that he'd had any intention of entering the store via his car. All he wanted to do was sit in the car and listen to the radio. But then he accidentally put the car in reverse and hit the gas. The next thing he knew, he plowed through four cars in the parking lot and gone through the store. Someone clearly needs to tell Arturo that in most cars made in the last 40 years, you can listen to the radio without actually starting the engine.

No one was hurt (except the store window). Arturo was cited for careless driving. And we suspect he may not be taken on any more shopping trips. (Which means, of course, that he *won*.)

Source: Local10.com

WHAT? NO KID NAMED
AFTER COLONEL TOM PARKER?

Now, we like Elvis as much as anyone—we prefer the young Elvis to the heftier Vegas version, but despite our appreciation of the 1968 comeback special and *Jailhouse Rock* alike, we have our obsession under control.

Not so Jean-Pierre and Carine Antheunis, of Gent, Belgium. They have a little bit of an Elvis *thing*. Every time they have a child, they name the kid something that has something to do with Elvis. So, some of their kids' names: Elvis (of course), Priscilla, Tennessee, and Dakota. We're not sure what Dakota has to do with Elvis (although we know he's frequently rumored to be working in a convenience store in South Dakota). Just remember, we *like* Elvis. We don't *live* Elvis.

Alas, the Antheunis couple have a problem. They had fifteen kids(!), but then they had number sixteen—a boy—and they plumb run out of Elvis-related names. "If it had been a girl we would have called her Linda. Elvis once had a lover with that name," said Jean-Pierre. Now we could offer obscure Elvis-related suggestions—how about Charro?—but the Antheunis appear to have settled on "Ohio" as a name. "There's no connection with Elvis, but it's in America," Jean-Pierre said. Well, don't forget the Rock and Roll Hall of Fame is there.

It could have been worse. They could have named their kids after Duran Duran's songs.

Source: Ananova, *Beacon-Journal* (Akron, OH)

MAYBE CATERING NEXT TIME?

Pity poor Nikolai, from Todiresti, Romania. While most men look forward to a home-cooked meal prepared by their loving wives, Nikolai dreaded each and every one. Nikolai, you see, believed his wife to be perhaps the worst cook that ever lived—the Wolfgang Puck of bad cooks, if you will. Apparently, there was no dish she couldn't prepare horribly.

In time, it seems, Nikolai's dread of his wife's cooking sublimated into another vector of emotion entirely: anger at the kitchen that enabled Nikolai's wife to create meal after terrifying meal. Something had to be *done*. The kitchen needed to be *stopped*. And so it was that Nikolai entered the kitchen, opened up the valve on the gas, and then, at the right moment, threw a match on the stove. Take that, Dread Kitchen of Evil!

The room exploded, naturally enough, and Nikolai learned that when you play with fire, you're going to get burned—he injured his hand in the explosion. Nikolai would later tell police that his inspiration for the explosion came from the action films of Arnold Schwarzenegger and Bruce Willis, although we're personally hard-pressed to remember a scene in which either of them exacted revenge on a kitchen.

Nikolai was charged with destruction of property and endangering the life of his wife. He could get three years for that. But since that's three years Nikolai won't have to eat his wife's cooking, we're guessing he won't see that as being an entirely bad thing.

Source: Ananova, *Seattle Times*

A NEW SPIN ON THE "SHOTGUN WEDDING"

Clem" was excited about the wedding—and we celebrate that emotion. That's the way you're supposed to feel when you're a groomsman and helping your good buddy take that transition into married life. But there are appropriate ways to show that emotion. A witty toast at the reception. A nice gift. A bachelor party that will be remembered for years. All of these, acceptable. Firing off a semi-automatic weapon in a wedding limo? Not so much.

Panicked driver reports of shots being fired out of the sport utility-type limos brought the Macomb County, Michigan, sheriffs' cars bearing down on the two wedding limos. The cops made all thirty-four members of the wedding party pile out of the cars—including the bride and groom. They searched the cars for the unconventional noisemaker, which they found in the form of a Glock pistol. Clem admitted the gun was his but swore he didn't fire it, which was strange, since the cops determined the gun had recently been fired. What's more, they found evidence to suggest the gun had been stolen.

Thirty-three members of the wedding party were allowed to pile back into the limos and go on to their wedding revelry. Clem, on the other hand, was arrested and charged with receiving and concealing a stolen firearm, violating concealed weapons laws, and firing from a vehicle. That was worth a $25,000 bond, which Clem forfeited when he skipped bail.

Oh, Clem. Next time, just try a nice toast.

Source: *Detroit Free Press,* Clickondetroit.com

A FISHY DOMESTIC DISPUTE

The man claimed to the Michigan State Police trooper that his girlfriend had assaulted him with a knife. And the evidence appeared to back him up: there were cuts all over his body, as well a bite wound on his shoulder. The knife was not suspected to be the culprit of the bite wound. But everything else looked blade inflicted.

The girlfriend admitted to chewing on her boyfriend— a retaliatory bite, apparently, as she claimed he bit first—but denied she had so much as touched her man with a knife. When pressed on the subject, however the women divulged the unusual instrument of stabination:

A fish.

Yes, apparently, this charming couple had been whacking on each other for some amount of time, and it appeared as if the guy was going to get the upper hand. Then our heroine, showing the resourcefulness of a mother cougar defending her young—or at least of a future Jerry Springer show candidate readying herself for her moment of syndication—reached up to grab a mounted, stuffed fish from the mantle of the fireplace, and then proceeded to whale upon her boyfriend. We assume the guy told the cop he'd been stabbed with a knife because admitting to being perforated by a fish would make him look like a chump.

The girlfriend was hauled away, but we wonder what the charges might have been. Assault with a deadly, dead fish?

Source: Associated Press

Dim Bulbs in Bright Lights
WAYNE'S WORLD (1992)

Our Dumb Guys: Wayne Campbell (Mike Myers) and Garth Algar (Dana Carvey)

Our Story: Two guys living genial but dead-end lives do a local access cable show from a basement in Aurora, Illinois. A sleazy ad executive (a brilliantly cast Rob Lowe) offers them big money to upgrade the show and take on a sponsor, but our boys soon learn that corporate ties are the ties that bind. Along the way, lots of big hair metal music gets played, some of it by Wayne's girlfriend (Tia Carrera).

Dumb or Stoned? A number of Wayne and Garth's friends clearly partake of beer and other intoxicants, but the heroes themselves are largely clean. Also, neither Wayne or Garth are morons, they're just easily entertained and a bit clueless (such as when they sign away the rights to their show for a few thousand dollars).

High Point of Low Comedy: The lip-synced performance of Queen's "Bohemian Rhapsody" in Garth's car is one of the best moments of young adult working-class humor of the 1990s, but the *Scooby Doo* surprise ending is the cleverest bit by far.

And Now, In Their Own Words: Wayne describing his year-long illness: "I once thought I had mono for an entire year. It turned out I was just really bored."

They're Dumb, But Is the Film Good? It's highly amusing by it's own merits, and as far as films based on sketches from *Saturday Night Live* go, it's really in a class by itself. *Cone-heads* and *A Night at the Roxbury* would make Wayne and Garth hurl.

CHAPTER 18

TiPS FOR STUPID CRIMINALS

We hear you ask: are you really giving more tips to stupid criminals? Aren't law-abiding citizens suffering enough? So, just to be safe, for all you stupid criminals out there, the following tips are for entertainment purposes only. Please do not follow them. If you should continue with criminal activities, please do so in as stupid a manner as possible, so that you will be easily caught and then safely locked up. Thank you for your attention. Now, on to the stories . . .

TiP 1
DON'T LEAVE A PAPER TRAIL

Sam" and "Paul" knew this about cash registers:** just as cracking a walnut's hard outer shell yields the nutty goodness inside, so will the cash register issue forth green wads of cash and metal discs of change. This money goodness is why the industrious duo kicked in the door of that Austin, Minnesota, restaurant, wrenched the shop's cash register from its moorings, and fled the scene just as they were spotted by a passing cab driver, who called the cops to report their adventure.

What Sam and Paul apparently didn't realize is that money is not all that a cash register stores. Some models (including the model they stole) also store long rolls of paper used to print out receipts for the customers. How long are these rolls of paper? Well, their lengths do vary, but in this particular case, it was just long enough that police called to the scene of the crime noticed that it had slipped out from the register, and followed its trail into the nearby bushes. Whereupon they found Sam, Paul, and the cash register, all in very close proximity to each other.

Sam and Paul were arrested, of course. Hopefully they'll get a receipt with their charges.

Source: Associated Press

TIP 2
DON'T FORGET ABOUT
THE DYE PACK

And what's the dye pack? See, when you rob a bank, while the teller is shoveling cash into a bag, he or she will also slip in a contraption that looks like a regular wad of bills but actually contains an exploding canister filled with colored paint. When the canister explodes shortly after the perp leaves the scene, both he or she and the stolen money will be covered in paint, which makes a thief difficult to overlook and the money even harder to spend.

"Sandra," who missed "Exploding Dye Pack 101" at bank robbing school, learned about the dye the hard way on the day that she walked into a Fort Worth, Texas, bank and robbed it. The teller handed over a bag filled with wads of cash and also a dye pack. Sandra grabbed the bag, left the scene, and overlooked the telltale canister hidden in her loot.

What does one do with a huge pile of ill-gained cash? In Sandra's case, and in apparent obliviousness to the irony of such an action, she drove to the town of Burleson to deposit the cash in *another* bank where, much to her surprise, the dye pack exploded just as she tried to deposit the money. Covered in pink paint, Sandra figured out real quick that the jig was up. She and her stolen wads of cash, now also a warm shade of pink, fled the scene but were picked up a short while later by local law enforcement who had no problem finding her because, after all, she was painted pink.

Source: Reuters

TIP 3
DON'T BE EARLY
TO YOUR ROBBERY

Perhaps "Erik" had other things on his agenda for the day besides robbing the bank and wanted to get an early start on his larceny. This might be why he showed up at that bank in Arendal, Norway, at 8:30 in the morning, swathed in a balaclava-type hood and wielding a butcher knife.

Here's the thing, though; the bank didn't open until 9 a.m. The door was locked while the bank personnel went through their early-morning activities. So there's Erik, in his balaclava and with his knife, standing at the door, waiting to get in. And what does he do next? *He knocks on the door.* To be let in.

Well, naturally, this doesn't work terribly well. See, if you are a person working at a bank, no matter how much you pride yourself on the refreshing, helpful personal service you provide to each and every customer, chances are pretty good that you're not going to be in a huge rush to admit into your place of business a knife-wielding fellow wearing a mask. And if you are, you should be fired.

Now what's Erik to do? At this point, the prudent thing for a weapon-wielding potential robber to do is run away, ditch the knife and balaclava, and try to get through the rest of the day without attracting any attention to yourself. But Erik had a better idea. He was early, sure. So he'd just wait. For the bank to open. Then he could *conduct his business.* So that's what he did, stationing himself and his knife on a nearby bench, which is where the police found and arrested him shortly thereafter.

So remember, you crazy, larcenous kids: early to bed and early to rise may make a man healthy, wealthy, and wise. Early to a robbery just gets you in trouble.

Source: *Aftenposten*

TIP 4
AiR VENTS AND CRIMINALS DON'T MIX

It was an early Sunday morning in the U.S. Virgin Islands town of Christiansted, but "Adrian" was not having a day of rest—indeed, far from it, as he was busy robbing himself a cafe and trying to find a way to open the store's safe. Before he could figure it out, however, the cafe's morning shift arrived, slightly earlier than usual. Trapped, Adrian looked to hide and ended up stuffing himself very tightly into the cafe's air conditioning vent.

This would have been a fine idea, had not the staff then decided to turn on the AC. For once they did, Adrian couldn't help but notice that the cooling system's fan was smacking him repeatedly and cutting into his flesh. And it was in the coiled-up, progressively minced position that the cafe's staff found him a few minutes later, as they followed up the strange sounds coming from the cooling system.

Adrian got a trip to the hospital. Then he got a trip to jail. Maybe he should have made it a day of rest after all.

Source: Associated Press

TiP 5
KNOW YOUR TECHNOLOGY

Bud" and "Jan" wanted a Cadillac sold by an Indepen-
dence, Missouri, dealership. They just weren't keen on
paying for it. Since stealing one was the only way, they nabbed
a sweet model, one equipped with the OnStar navigation system. Not only could OnStar tell them how to get places, it
could also let the dealership know where the stolen vehicle
was being taken. But Bud and Jan (who by all indications had
done their research on the make and model of car with which
they were absconding) were prepared; shortly after they stole
the car, they ripped out the car's antenna—thereby silencing
the onboard tracking system.

Or so they thought. What they had actually done was rip
out the antenna for the Caddie's XM satellite radio service. So
while the Caddie could no longer get dozens of channels of
CD-quality musical entertainment beamed to it from the cold,
hard vacuum of space, it *could* still rat on Bud and Jan. Which
is what it did and which is how police tracked down Bud and
Jan later that same day.

David Clutts, executive manager of the dealership from
which the Caddie was stolen, summed up Bud and Jan's problem to the local newspaper: "They're like most people who commit stupid crimes. They didn't know what they were doing."

Source: *The Examiner* (Eastern Jackson County, MO)

TIP 6
KNOW THE LAW
IN YOUR JURISDICTION

Rob" had decided he's had enough of the life of a free man. He was broke, unable to find work, and to top it all off, abandoned by his wife. Depressed, he decided to end it all. Not by *dying*, but by robbing a bank in Yakima, Washington. See, back in California, Rob had three armed robbery convictions; he figured another one would trigger Washington state's "Three Strikes" law and then he would have to be sentenced to life in prison. While life in prison is generally understood *not* to be a big bundle of fun, Rob figured it was free room and board; at the very least, he wouldn't have to worry about what his social schedule would be like for the next several decades. So Rob went into that Yakima bank, robbed it, then took a seat, and waited for the cops to arrive. He figured he was a lifer for sure.

Guess again, Rob! It seems that thanks to a bizarre quirk in the way Washington's Three Strikes law works, Rob's California convictions only counted as one strike against him in Washington state. So even though Rob the Robber had robbed on four separate occasions (that we know about), in the eyes of the great state of Washington, they only counted as two strikes. So Rob's felonious gesture wasn't good enough for a lifetime of prison food and surly guards.

He had to content himself with a consolation prize—er, *sentence*—of "just" eight and a half years. But maybe if he's lucky the state will deny him parole! We can all hope.

Source: Associated Press

TIP 7
PSSST ... THEY CAN SEE
YOU ON THE INTERNET

Down in the Dallas, Texas, suburb of Garland, members of two gangs of intemperate rapscallions—let's call them "The Ruffians" and "The Cads"—started taunting each other with rather nasty strings of messages on Internet chat rooms associated with their music heroes. Given the shocking profanity of the messages, we can't actually recount them here, so allow us to offer this re-enactment with language from a more gentle and civilized time:

> **Ruffian Member:** I say! It is well known among people of class and distinction that the members of The Cads are no more than errant knaves!
>
> **Cad Member:** Why, you base spouter of vile untruths! I shall strike you about the pate!
>
> **Ruffian Member:** Indeed you shall not, for I and my band of good fellows shall strike blows upon you, and cause you much shame and discomfort!
>
> **Cad Member:** 'Tis not so, you conniving wretch! Name but a time and place, and The Cads shall be there and you shall receive your richly deserved thrashing!

And so it came to pass that The Ruffians and The Cads *did* decide to have a rumble, and used the Internet to pass along information about time and place. This came in handily after the brawl when members of the Garland Police Department started looking online for information about the incident. Their investigations led them to the chat rooms where the gang members were sniping at each other; as some of the gang members had signed in with their own names, they were reasonably easy to track down.

Garland police eventually nabbed nearly three dozen people—most high school students—who were suspected of being present at the brawl, and charged them with a variety of offenses including riot participation and serious bodily injury, a felony that can get you up to twenty years. Additional evidence was supplied through a videotape one gang member made of the brawl. If you've gone through the trouble of announcing your brawl online, then why *not* tape it? As a bonus, you can stream the video afterwards!

Intemperate rapscallions!

Source: Associated Press

TIP 8
MAKE SURE YOUR FAKE BADGE DOESN'T SAY SOMETHING STUPID

In the first *Book of the Dumb,* we recounted the tale of a man who thought it would be fun to pretend to be a cop and pull people over on the road—and maybe it was, until he pulled over an off-duty cop who proceeded to show him what an actual cop thinks about the fake kind.

Sadly, "Josh," of Hobe Sound, Florida, must not have been given a copy of the first book for a birthday or major gift-giving holiday, because he tried pulling the same stunt; one night off of I-95, Josh flashed the realistic-looking lights of his car to pull over a female driver. The bad news for him was that she happened to be an off-duty Palm Beach Sheriff's deputy; what was even worse news for Josh was that the female deputy had a male deputy friend following her in another car. So suddenly, there were three people with badges—but two of them had real badges, and Josh wasn't either of those two.

What gave Josh away? Well, for one thing, the lights on his vehicle weren't correct—a little detail that few outside law enforcement would have picked up. However, even the least aware people might have suspected Josh's badge was fake, as in addition to identifying him as "Miami Vice" (which if nothing else meant he was out of his jurisdiction), it also proclaimed him to be an inspector of the female reproductive system (although of course the badge described it rather less politely). His badge number: "69." Yeah, that's not a badge that exactly screams credibility.

What happens when you play at being a cop with real cops? They practice a little arrestitude on you: Josh was charged with impersonating an officer.

Source: TheSmokingGun.com. TCPalm.com, The *Palm Beach Post*

TiP 9
JUST TAKE THE WALLET
AND RUN

There are three criminals in our story, and the three of them ganged up on some poor fellow at the Solingen-Ohligs train stop in Düsseldorf, Germany, and forced the schmoe to give them his wallet. From said wallet they extracted cash. In a token gesture (of what, we don't know), one of thieves returned the empty wallet to the fellow they just robbed, perhaps to show that they weren't *complete* thieving jerks, or the better for him to fill it up again to be robbed at a later time (it's the miscreant's ATM!). A better strategy would have just been to take the wallet and hightail it out of there.

Why, do you ask? Well, because when the robber with a heart of gold handed the victim a wallet, it wasn't the victim's wallet—it was the robber's. That lovely billfold contained within it the robber's identification, just the kind of information the police love to have when tracking down a criminal! The thief was then quickly rounded up by the cops, who, after all, knew where he lived. His pals were picked up later. (No word if the victim actually ever got the right wallet back.) So thieves, keep your wallet on you or that might be the last mugging you'll ever pull.

Source: Ananova

TIP 10
HEY BIG SPENDER,
TRY LAYING LOW FOR A WHILE

Yes, that's right. You knocked over that bank. Very nice. However, if you're then spending like a swell an hour later, how does that look? Right, it looks like someone might try to get some reward money out of turning you in.

"Albert" held up a Wilmington, North Carolina, branch of the Bank of America. The robbery went as robberies do, and Albert exited the bank shortly after 4 p.m. *Just a few minutes later,* Albert pops up at a nearby bar, carrying a duffel bag, a bus ticket, and a bunch of $100 bills, that he uses to buy drinks, make big tips, and call a whole lot of attention to himself. Al's profligacy may have been a significant contributing factor to someone ratting him out to the cops a few hours later, once footage from the robbery made the rounds in the local media.

By the time the cops rolled into the bar, Albert had lit out—but later, the cops got a call about a home invasion, and it was our pal Al. Apparently he'd tried to placate the people whose house he had broken into by announcing "I've got money"; strangely, the people confronted with a stranger in their home were not impressed. Al then tried to hoof away, but he didn't get very far. He was charged with armed robbery and first-degree burglary and held under $100,000 bail. He should have just spent a quiet evening at home.

Source: Associated Press, Wilmington Police Department

TIP 11
DON'T MOON OVER
YOUR SENTENCE

Yeah, okay, we'll admit it, who *doesn't* like a grand, irrational gesture of defiance every once in a while? But as the Bible and The Byrds have told us, to everything there is a season: a time to laugh, a time to cry, a time to sow, a time to reap, a time to act foolishly and a time to wear a suit, stand in front of a judge and admit your foolishness in a grave and dignified manner. All right, they don't say that last bit *exactly,* but they *should.*

"Lee" wasn't buying the dignified matter strategy. In front of Connecticut judge Patrick Carroll, he was supposed to plead guilty to armed robbery and conspiracy to commit robbery as part of a plea bargain. Judge Carroll told Lee to address him as "Sir," and Lee, to his credit, did. But rather *not* to his credit, he did it in the context of saying, "Sir? Kiss my [insert salty expression for posterior here], sir!" and then dropping his pants and waving his cheeks at the now-affronted jurist.

It'll be a great story to tell in the prison yard, for sure. Judge Carroll made sure that Lee would get an opportunity to try it out as soon as possible: he slapped Lee with a six-month prison term for contempt of court. Oh, and that plea bargain? Yeah, Lee could forget about *that* too. In all, Lee's few seconds of cheek-flapping will probably cost him an extra five and a half years. It's not what we would call a good trade.

Source: Associated Press

TiP 12
THE POLICE HANG OUT
AT THE COURTHOUSE

Kevin" **caught a break** that day he was pulled over for a traffic stop with drugs in his car. He was arrested; but then, a search warrant executed at his house found eight guns he, as a former felon, shouldn't have had and a meth lab. And you ask, so how is this lucky? Well, Kevin was held during all this without actually being charged with anything—and since he hadn't been charged within a specified period of time, he was sprung from jail before charges could be filed (which they later were—making Kevin a wanted man). The average crook would have seen this as divine providence and gotten out of Dodge before the authorities could catch up to him.

Not Kevin. He not only didn't run, he actually showed up at the courthouse about a week later. Why? Well, remember that traffic stop that was the start of his woes? Those charges were what he had come to settle. Perhaps he thought that if he could get those charges taken care of or dismissed, all the other stuff would go away too.

The sheriff's deputy recognized Kevin, who was arrested and charged this time with manufacturing methamphetamines and having a weapon under disability (which means having guns when you're not supposed to). Kevin shouldn't count on divine providence bailing him out a second time.

Source: *Times-Recorder* (Zanesville, OH)

TIP 13
TRY KNOCKING FIRST

Vince" probably figured that **no one was home** in that nice Jackson, Mississippi, house he planned to burgle. After all, there was no car in the driveway. No car at the house means everyone's gone, right?

Vince parked his own car in the driveway, went up to the front door, kicked it, and peered through the crack the kicks had opened. At which point he saw the owner of the house, a professional security guard, pointing and shooting a .38-caliber revolver at him three times. So much for the whole "no cars = no people in the house" theory.

It seems that being shot at and hit at least once turned his mind rather quickly from larceny to velocity. In all the confusion and gunfire, Vince fled so quickly that he quite forgot his still-running car parked in the driveway, a beautiful gift to the cops, for sure.

Later Vince showed up at a local hospital, claiming he'd just been walking down the street minding his own business when a bullet came out of nowhere and whacked his finger. The cops, on the case after the homeowner called in the breaking and entering, chose not to buy the "mysterious bullet" theory and issued a warrant for his arrest. That's what you get for sticking your nose—and head, and hands—into houses it doesn't belong. Truly, a lesson for us all.

Source: *Clarion-Ledger* (Jackson, MS)

TIP 14
THOU SHALT NOT STEAL—
ESPECIALLY FROM GOD

Anyone who steals is definitely taking their chances. As the saying goes, there are no atheists in foxholes, so we bet that thieves can be a pretty pious lot at times too. Muttering a quick prayer right before a job might sway the Supreme Being to overlook a criminal act or two. So we can't for the life of us figure out why these two dolts decided to make the Man Upstairs angry. If you've ever read the Old Testament, you know you wouldn't like him when he's angry.

"Hugh" and "Drew" decided that stealing from a church would be a grand idea. The collections box at Chicago's West Side Catholic Church seemed pretty easy pickings to them. In fact, they figured it'd be so easy they didn't really need to hide their intentions. The two sauntered up to the locked collection box, laid out their church-money-stealing tools, and then went right to work.

But in this case, not only was God watching, but so was Father Matt Foley. Since the church had been robbed before, the priest had seen fit to put a video surveillance camera on the contribution box. On seeing the sinners, Father Foley rushed out to confront them and attempted to take away their tools. Hugh, not to be dissuaded from his prize by a priest proclaimed to all and sundry that he had a knife. Father Foley, less than impressed, grabbed the man, got him in a half-nelson, and had him kissing ground in no time flat. And that's where the cops, summoned by parishioners, found Foley and

Hugh (they later captured Drew). Turns out that Father Foley, although a man of peace by calling, had grown up with six siblings. That'll teach you to fight, all right.

Father Foley served notice that he'd be ready to wrestle the next would-be thief to the ground as well, and told reporters, "No one steals from God." At least, not in his church.

Source: cbs2chicago.com

TIP 15
KEEP IT DOWN

How many people does it take to rob a pizza delivery guy? In Springfield, Massachusetts, the answer is apparently six because that's how many miscreants popped up to rob the Pizza Works delivery guy of his cash and about $45 worth of food and sodas. They had called in the order to a neutral location, set on the poor delivery guy, and then headed to parts unknown.

Just not unknown for long. One of the robbers dropped a scarf at the robbery scene, which provided a clue for Springfield's K9 crew. The dogs sniffed a trail back to a building down the road. But the real clue that the robbers were inside came not from the dogs, but from the robbers themselves in a second-story apartment, who could be heard arguing—loudly—about how to split up the take. This is just one reason why getting six people in on a pizza robbery isn't very smart: six people have enough problems just splitting a pizza, let alone a pizza robbery. Two of the guys then left the apartment and walked out of the door still arguing about the loot, which made it nice and easy for the cops, who were just standing there, to arrest them. They found in the apartment: money, a gun, and food matching the order called in for the robbery.

"We're just happy that these guys are dumber and greedier than we are," said Springfield Police Capt. William J. Noonan. Not to mention louder.

Source: Court TV

The Annals of Ill-Advised Television

TODAY'S EPISODE: COP ROCK

Starring in this Episode: Ronny Cox and Paul McCrane

Debut Episode: September 26, 1990, on ABC

The Pitch: It's just like *Hill Street Blues,* except that every few minutes everyone bursts into song. No, really; creator Steven Bochco got the idea for the series when it was suggested that his previous hit series *Hill Street Blues* should be made into a Broadway musical. He passed on that idea (which is kind of a shame) and ran with this instead.

It Seemed Like a Good Idea at the Time Because: Well, because Steven Bochco, at the time, had a fabulous track record in creating popular, quirky series like *L.A. Law,* and *Doogie Howser, M.D.* It also probably helped that noted songwriter Randy Newman was signed on to write some of the series' songs, including the theme song "Under the Gun." If anyone could make the idea of a musical cop drama work, it was these two.

In Reality: Surprise! Not even these two could make it work. ABC, in hock to the show to the tune of nearly $2 million an episode (a record for the time), tried advertising the show in movie theaters; the trailer got snickers and boos. Viewers were appalled from the first episode, which featured a courtroom scene in which the jury sang "He's Guilty" to the defendant as if it were a gospel choir.

How Long Did It Last? Eleven episodes, with the final one (entitled "Bang the Potts Slowly") airing the night after Christmas. In an interesting bit of irony, more than a decade later musical numbers in TV series became all the rage, the most famous example being the celebrated "Once More With Feeling" episode of *Buffy, The Vampire Slayer.* It should be noted, however, that with the exception of *The Simpsons* (which can get away with anything), no network show since *Cop Rock* has made musical numbers a persistent, recurring feature.

Were Those Responsible Punished? Not so much. Bochco rebounded quickly with *NYPD Blue,* a traditional-if-racy cop show begun in 1993 that is still running as of this writing. Star Paul McCrane also chucked the music for a several-season stint on *ER,* while Ronny Cox went back into character acting in films and television. Randy Newman, of course, made oodles writing sardonic songs for Pixar films and even nabbed an Oscar for *Monsters, Inc.* We're still waiting for our *Hill Street Blues* Broadway musical, by the way.

CHAPTER 19

TRAVEL TRAVAILS

A wise man once said that no matter where you go, there you are. But a wise man also said that some times the journey is the destination. Combine these two sayings and it explains why it seems like you end up spending most of your life in an airport terminal. Now, we're not wise, but we do know this much: when one travels hundreds or even thousands of miles, each mile is an opportunity to do something really dumb. So celebrate the folks in the following stories for taking the initiative and crafting a dumb experience we all can share.

NAPTIME AT 36,000 FEET

Let's begin by noting that the very best time for a commercial airline pilot to take a nap is sometime when he or she is not actually in the air. It's just a crazy little thing we've got going, but when we entrust our lives to a human being piloting a multiton conveyance carrying ourselves and a couple hundred other people six miles above the surface of the planet and supported only by a nice stiff breeze, we prefer that human to be *conscious* for most—indeed, all—of that trip.

Having said that, pilots who feel the compelling need to get a little shut-eye mid-flight are nevertheless well advised not to take the example of "Hiro," a pilot for the Japanese All Nippon Airlines. Hiro was piloting eighty passengers from Tokyo to the city of Ube when he decided that it would be a fine time to studiously examine the inside of his eyelids. The autopilot was on, and his copilot appeared sufficiently alert, so, you know, why not?

One compelling reason why not: the official from Japan's Transportation Ministry, on board for a routine inspection, might view a dozing pilot as an issue for the airline. The official noticed the pilot slumbering and made mention of it to the copilot, who nudged the pilot awake. A few minutes later, the pilot was out again. This time his copilot, politeness be damned, actually did yell at him.

Hiro was grounded pending an investigation, and we suspect a fair number of Japanese started boarding flights with extra capsules of the Japanese version of No-Doz. As a gift for the pilot. Just in case.

Source: Sapa-AP

THINGS NOT TO LEAVE
IN YOUR RENTAL CAR

People leave lots of stuff in rental cars: partially eaten food, umbrellas, books, the occasional stuffed animal or a CD still stuffed in the in-dash player. But eighty-eight bags of heroin? Yeah, that's a new one on us.

And apparently a new one to the employees of Enterprise Rent-a-Car in Langhorne, Pennsylvania, who found the bags of the narcotic hidden under a layer of napkins (so *that's* why the driver forgot them). Wisely, the employees did not use their discovery as seed capital for an ill-advised career switch into drug running, but instead called the police; in addition to the heroin, the employees also handed over something that they figured might come in handy in helping the cops track down the drugs' owner: the guy's wallet. Yes, our guy left behind his wallet and eighty-eight bags of heroin. Man, that's one forgetful dude.

The cops called "Jerry," the alleged drug-transporting wallet-leaver, and posing as lowlifes, offered to exchange the drugs for $300. Jerry agreed. When he showed up to take delivery, he was arrested and charged with possession of a controlled substance with intent to deliver.

Ironically, Jerry had been released from prison just a few months before. What was he in the slammer for? Heroin distribution. Dumb people never learn.

Source: Associated Press

AiRPORT INSECURITY

Shelia" the stripper was inebriated, scantily clad, and **sleepy.** So what did Sheila do? Since she wasn't at home, she decided to find a nice quiet spot to take a nap.

Now before you start pointing your fingers, let us inform you that her being drunk, sleepy, and a stripper is not the dumb part of the story. The dumb part of the story is that the cozy spot our heroine decided to nap in was an airplane. To get to it, she had to climb over a barbed wire fence (try that in a g-string!) at the Aberdeen Airport in Scotland without being detected by airport security. She had been in the airplane for *eight hours* before someone finally figured out she was there.

"I expect this incident causes great embarrassment to the airport authorities," security expert David Capitanchik noted to the BBC. "It's not the sort of thing that should happen. That's what barbed wire fences are there for and CCTV (closed circuit television) and guys who should be patrolling the perimeter."

Even Shelia was outraged. "If I can break into a major airport," she said, "what chance have they got catching terrorists?" Indeed. Especially since the terrorists are unlikely to be wearing such skimpy outfits.

Shelia was let off with a warning and banned from the airport—unless she's actually planning to fly somewhere. Although we suspect she's not going to be too keen on going anywhere from that particular airport. After all, she knows how lax security there can be.

Source: BBC, Reuters

IN MAN VS. TRAIN, BET ON THE TRAIN

"Charley" had an excellent reason to be irritated at trains. In 1989 the Appleton, Wisconsin, man had a run-in with a train that crushed his car and put him in a wheelchair. But that's not the reason that Charley hated locomotives. Fact is, he thought their horns are just too loud. And to protest their intrusion into his earspace, he would go right up to the tracks, where he could be seen by the engineers and conductors, and shoot them the bird. The train crews were so familiar with his presence they considered him a "regular," just another attraction on the trip. If it's a man in a wheelchair sticking up his middle finger, it must be Appleton.

One night Charley was preparing to flip off the Canadian National engine that was chugging down the track. But Charley's enthusiasm to get the best position apparently caused him to forget a critical thing: don't get too close to the train. Charley's wheelchair was clipped by the engine's gas tank. The collision sent Charley flying backward. Luckily, his only injuries were a mere scrape on his arm and a bruised ego.

Charley's reward for getting clipped? A citation from the Appleton police for being a pedestrian in violation of traffic signals. He was also advised to find a less dangerous way to register his complaints. That's probably good advice. Although if he takes it, how will the train crews know they're in Appleton?

Source: *The Post-Crescent* (Appleton, WI), USA Today

STEP OUTSIDE,
THEN FREE FALL

Larry" was like many vacationers to sunny Spain. He enjoyed his imbibibles. Although perhaps more than other vacationers—he enjoyed them so much that he would sometimes drink enough to make him surly and combative. As he was after he had downed most of a bottle of vodka and then decided to pick a fight with another vacationer. The details of why the particular fight was started are hazy, but we do know that Larry at one point went up to a man and asked him to "step outside" for a fight.

We know for fact that the two of them did not step outside. We know this because "outside" in this case was 25,000 feet up: Larry and his erstwhile opponent were passengers in an EasyJet flight from Alicante to Bristol. Larry was apparently so drunk that he didn't realize that "Let's you and me step outside" actually meant a freefall to certain death for both of them.

Larry discovered what being drunk and belligerent and vertically unaware can cost you: he was sentenced to three months in prison by the Bristol Crown Court, which said to him, "This sort of behaviour will not be tolerated on an aircraft." Exactly right. He should have waited until he was inside the terminal.

A hint for Larry, don't ask any of your new prison friends to "step outside." You won't have a 25,000-foot buffer zone to protect you then.

Source: *The Scotsman* (Scotland), *The Sun* (UK)

EMPTY VESSELS

We think it's a fine thing if the people who work for the Transportation Security Administration are a curious lot. They are charged with keeping America's airplanes safe and secure—and for a job like that it helps to wonder if a belt buckle is hiding a little knife or if someone's shoes just might have soles made out of explosives. So, yes, curious TSA agents get a big thumbs up from us, just as long as their curiosity doesn't involve *us* having to get a full body-cavity search.

On the other hand, we think that the TSA screeners should focus their curiosity on things that are materially relevant to their jobs. So as an example, "Gee, I wonder if I should put that guy's carrying case through the X-ray machine to see what's in it?" is an excellent use of TSA screener curiosity. "Gee, I wonder if I should put my own head through the X-ray machine to see what's in it?" is not.

But it was the latter sort of curiosity that gripped several TSA security screeners at a number of different airports. Who can blame them? Aren't we *all* curious about our own bodies, especially the parts we can't usually see without exposing ourselves to serious bodily harm? And here were the TSA screeners, in full control of X-ray machines. It was only natural that sooner or later some of them would pass themselves through the machines, as these several screeners did—they just slid themselves on the conveyor belts and rolled on in. The X-ray machines, 30 inches high and 18 inches wide, were big enough that they slipped through without problem. They didn't have to get a doctor's permission or anything.

Ah, but they *did* need to get the TSA's permission, a small detail that eluded these screeners. Here's what happens when you don't: the TSA confirmed in February 2004 that several of its screeners had been placed on administrative leave for passing themselves through the machines. Mike Fierberg, a TSA spokesman, denied to a Denver television station that passengers were ever put in danger because of the hi-jinx of the screeners, but he did allow that the TSA screeners' going through the X-ray machines themselves was pretty stupid— not to mention curious—behavior, and not in the good sense.

Source: KUSA-TV

REPORT THE NEWS,
DON'T MAKE IT

Here's a lesson we think is valuable for every pilot: top off the tank before you take to the sky. There may be things in life that are more unpleasant than running out of gas when the only thing between you and the ground are a few lucky updrafts, but they are few and we don't actually want to spend any time imagining what they are.

Topping off the fuel tank also might make you look a bit less foolish than the pilot and reporter in the KCBS Sky Three, a Cessna 172 used by the San Francisco radio station and other stations to monitor traffic in the Bay Area. We don't know that the pilot didn't fuel up before taking to the air that May 2004 morning, but we do know that at about 8:30 a.m., the plane's engine started sputtering, indicating that the tank was dry.

Well, you know what happens when a plane runs out of gas: gravity. The pilot looked for places to land and spotted a few school grounds, but in each case there were children on the grounds, and the pilot—wisely—decided that teaching the children the joys of playing with a falling Cessna should not be the lesson of the day.

That left the highway—itself not a bundle of fun at 8:30 on a weekday morning in the Bay Area. But the pilot managed, setting down on the Westbound 580 at the 238 split (i.e. traffic central). Then the plane, which was supposed to report on traffic slowdowns, created one as commuters gawked at the sight of the plane on the highway shoulder. At least there was a reporter on the scene to cover the news.

Source: *Chronicle* (San Francisco, CA), *Tri-Valley Herald*

WE'RE SORRY, THIS IS
A NO-SLAPPING FLIGHT

Try to follow this reasoning here, because we know it's got us a little confused. "Bobbi" was on a plane that was taxiing down the runway in Miami on its way to Philadelphia, and she was standing up, merrily chatting away on her cell phone to a friend. As anyone who has traveled by plane over the last few years knows, when a plane is just about ready for lift-off, they like you in your seat, and they like you not to be on your cell phone, which airline maintain can mess with cockpit communications.

So Bobbi was told—several times—by the flight attendants. Bobbi's response: "It is rude to hang up on people. I don't have to turn my phone off." Well, in fact, you do; it's a federal case if you interfere with a flight crew. Moreover, it's entirely likely the plane won't take off if someone is actively ignoring the flight crew. Strange as it may seem, it makes flight crews jumpy. So we ask you: what is more rude? Hanging up on a friend on your cell phone? Or inconveniencing an entire plane because you simply won't shut up? See, that's what we think, too. But not Bobbi.

The flight crew having been defeated by Bobbi's obnoxiousness decided it was time for the air marshals on the flight to tell her what to do. One of them told her to sit down, and put his hand on her shoulder to get her attention. Whereupon Bobbi slapped the air marshal smack in the face. We ask again: which is ruder? Hanging up your cell phone or physically assaulting a federal officer? Once again, we are in agreement. But, again, not Bobbi.

Sadly for Bobbi, this is when a bit of rudeness was visited upon her: she was taken down, handcuffed, hauled off the plane, and then charged with assaulting a federal officer and interfering with a flight crew. We wonder if she was allowed the customary phone call, seeing that she'd already been on the phone. But we guess that refusing her that call would be, you know, *rude*.

Source: Associated Press

DON'T RUSH ME

Something to know about a Coast Guard inspection of your merchant vessel, should you have a merchant vessel: it takes a while. Yes, as highly trained and efficient as the U.S. Coast Guard is in performing its duties, individually and severally, there is still an excellent chance that the performance of said duties will, in fact, consume quite a bit of time. Please find some way to amuse yourself until they are done. We hear solitaire is fun.

Our Turkish captain "Khamel" was apparently not a patient man. And so when the Coast Guard personnel from the Port of Philadelphia did not perform their duties in a manner that Khamel deemed timely, he struck upon an innovative strategy to speed them along when he blurted out that there was a bomb on board.

This did *not* speed things up. On the contrary, the Coast Guard ordered the ship back to sea, where rather than the quick inspection the Coast Guard had been performing, the ship got the full inspection treatment complete with bomb-sniffing dogs brought in for the occasion. Khamel, realizing he'd stupidly extended the time he had to wait before his ship could dock, tried to take back the comment, but as one Coast Guard official said, "He'd already rung the bell."

Khamel himself found another, exciting way to wait. He was detained by the FBI for making a false statement to a federal official, which is a felony. More proof that patience (and honesty!) is a virtue.

Source: NBC News, Delaware Online

TRAVEL TRAVAILS

One of the stories is a round trip ticket to Truthville. Two of them lead to an infinite layover in Falseburg. Which is which? Pick your choice and then board to discover your destination.

1. The skies are filled with stories of drunken passengers abusing flight attendants. But drunken flight attendants abusing passengers? That's a new one on us. And yet it happened—and perhaps stereotypically, it happened in Russia. It was there, on an Aeroflot flight from Moscow to Nizhnevartovsk, that the flight crew caused a scene, first by disappearing for most of the trip, then reappearing near the end of the trip to drunkenly pass out food to the passengers. One of the passengers complained about the service, and three of the male flight attendants took it upon themselves to give the guy several knuckle sandwiches and blacken his eye. The man, naturally enough, has filed a lawsuit against the airline, and the flight attendants are looking at three months each in a Russian prison. Have a nice trip, guys!

2. The Quantas flight from Los Angeles to Auckland was going along swimmingly, until somewhere over the Pacific, the plane's in-flight entertainment system gave out with six hours left to go until touchdown. This could have meant nothing but hours of staring at the South Pacific, but the

Qantas flight crew had another idea. "Robert [McGee, one of the flight crew] remembered that a passenger brought a guitar as her carry-on," said head attendant Sarah Nelson. McGee, it turns out, had been a guitarist for a wedding band in Australia. The result: hours of passenger-request singalong. "I'd been looking forward to watching *Bruce Almighty*," said 19-year-old Jane Stross, whose guitar had been borrowed. "But this was pretty cool, too."

3. As part of their in-flight entertainment options, many airlines allow their passengers to listen in to flight deck communication between the airline pilots and the air traffic controllers. The prospect of messing with some of those listeners proved to be irresistible to two Swiss International Air Lines pilots, who on a flight between Geneva and London decided to re-enact a famous episode of *The Twilight Zone* in which an equipment-destroying gremlin is spotted on the wing of the plane. It was a fine joke until that woman in the first class cabin who had been listening in freaked out and started screaming uncontrollably, forcing an emergency landing. Turns out the woman, who hated flying, had self-medicated prior to departure and was not in any mental position to distinguish reality from puckish pilot jokes. The after the plane's eventual arrival in London, the pilots were put on paid leave pending an airline and pilot's union investigation.

Turn to page 329 for the answers.

The Annals of Ill-Advised Television

TODAY'S EPISODE: SUPERTRAIN

Starring in this Episode: Robert Alda and Ilene Graff

Debut Episode: February 7, 1979, on NBC

The Pitch: It's *The Love Boat*! On rails! Apparently convinced that a nation that considers Amtrak as the transportation of absolute last resort would buy into the idea of a super-luxury train, NBC greenlit this one, in which the train, in gross violation of physical laws, features an Olympic-sized swimming pool, a mall, and a disco, and travels at 200 miles an hour.

It Seemed Like a Good Idea at the Time Because: Well, *The Love Boat* was a big hit at the time. Also, one of the creators of the series was noted novelist Donald E. Westlake, who by this time had several successful novels (and movie adaptations thereof) to his name.

In Reality: *The Love Boat* had apparently slaked the nation's thirst for traveling B-level celebrities (like Lyle Waggoner, Zsa Zsa Gabor, and Billy Barty) and amusing romantic adventures. There were also substantial production problems as well. Early on (in a bit of foreshadowing, perhaps?) the very expensive model of the Supertrain crashed while the show producers were showing it off to the NBC brass, which required an equally expensive alternate version to be constructed. The first five episodes rated so poorly that the show's executive producer was replaced; the new executive producer added cast members and—on episode nine—a laugh track, none of which seemed to do any good.

How Long Did It Last? Nine episodes, with the last airing on May 5, 1979—although NBC (likely out of programming desperation and to make back its money) played the show again during summer re-runs.

Were Those Responsible Punished? NBC programming head Fred Silverman would eventually lose his job for this and other bad series (see *Pink Lady . . . and Jeff* on page 94). Donald E. Westlake survived apparently unscathed and would later be nominated for an Oscar for his screenplay adaptation of *The Grifters*.